THE NUTCRACKER

Complete Ballet in Full Score

THE NUTCRACKER

Complete Ballet in Full Score

Peter Ilyitch
TCHAIKOVSKY

DOVER PUBLICATIONS
Garden City, New York

Bibliographical Note

This Dover edition, first published in 2004, is an unabridged republication of an authoritative early edition. Credits, contents, instrumentation, a glossary, and translations of French and Russian texts have all been newly added.

International Standard Book Number

ISBN-13: 978-0-486-43836-8
ISBN-10: 0-486-43836-8

Manufactured in the United States of America
43836815
www.doverpublications.com

Щелкунчик
Балет-Фээрия в 2-х Действиях

Casse-Noisette
Ballet-Féerie en 2 Actes

THE NUTCRACKER

Ballet in 2 Acts
Op. 71

Music by Peter Ilyitch Tchaikovsky
Composed February 1891–April 1892

Scenario by Marius Petipa and Ivan Vsevolozhsky
after Alexandre Dumas' *Histoire d'un Casse-Noisette* (1845),
adapted from E.T.A. Hoffmann's *Nußknacker und Mausekönig* (1816)

First performance:
18 December 1892, at the Mariinsky Theatre, St. Petersburg
Conducted by Riccardo Drigo
Choreography by Lev Ivanov

Sugar Plum Fairy: Antonietta dell'Era
Prince: Pavel Gerdt
Nutcracker: Sergei Legat

CONTENTS

Instrumentation

3 Flutes [Flauti]
Fl. III doubles Piccolo
2 Oboes [Oboi]
English Horn [Corno Inglese]
2 Clarinets [Clarinetti in B]
Bass Clarinet [Clarinetto Basso]
2 Bassoons [Fagotti]

4 Horns [Corni]
2 Trumpets [Trombe]
3 Trombones [Tromboni]
Tuba [Tuba]

Timpani [Timpani]
Triangle [Triangolo]
Bass Drum [Gran Cassa]
Cymbals [Piatti]
Rattle/Ratchet [Schnarre]
Tambourine [Tamburino]
Castanets [Castagnetti]
Tam-Tam [Tam-Tam]
Glockenspiel [Glockenspiel]

2 Harps [Arpe]
Celesta (or Piano) [Celesta (ou Piano)]

Violins [Violini]
Violas [Viole]
Cellos [Violoncelli]
Basses [Contrabassi]

Stage instruments:
Toy trumpets [Trompettes d'enfant]
Toy drums [Tambours d'enfant]
Various toy instruments [Instruments d'enfant]

Glossary of Russian Terms

(with French and German equivalents as they appear in the score)

Болш. Фл. / *Gr. Flöte.* = Flute

Детский барабанъ / *Tambour d'enfant* = Child's drum

За сценой = Off stage
Закр. зв. / *Gestopft* = Stopped
Занавѣсъ / *Rideau* = Curtain

И Т.Д. = Etc.

Кроличьихъ барабанчика / *Lapins à tambour* = Rabbit drummers

Мал. Фл. / *Piccolo* = Piccolo

На сцене / *Sur la scène* = On stage

Открыто / *Nicht gestopft* = Open

Палочкой / *Mit Paukenschlägel* = With stick
Пальцем по кожѣ / *Mit dem Daumen* = With the thumb on the drumhead
Предъидущаго = Preceding
Приготовить (1ю/2ю) мал. флейту / *Kleine Fl. (Piccolo) vorbereiten* = Prepare (1st/2nd) piccolo
Приготовить большую флейту / *Grosse Fl. vorbereiten* = Prepare flute
Просто / *Wie gewöhnlich* = Simply, as usual (*modo ord.*)

Снять сурдины = Remove mutes (*senza sordini*)

Трещётка / *Schnarre* = Rattle

Хоръ = Chorus
Хоръ 24хъ женскихъ или дѣтскихъ голосовъ = Chorus of 24 female or children's voices

Russian Notes in the Score

Page 96: (Somewhat more relaxed than the tempo before the preceding *Allegro vivo.*)

Page 115: These instruments are the same as those used in the first scene of *The Queen of Spades.* At the indicated places, the children on stage should play them.

Page 115: The RATTLE is the same instrument used in the Children's Symphonies of HAYDN, ROMBERG, etc. It can be obtained in almost any music store.

Page 130: NOTE. In addition to these two instruments, the children, in this place and subsequent places like it, may make noise with other instruments used in Children's Symphonies: cuckoos, quails, cymbals, etc. However, the rattle is not used here because it is already found in the orchestra and has been given other functions. The cuckoo and quail should be in the key of C major.

Page 137: Note: Repeated a few times *ad libitum.*

Page 170: (Two or more similar toy drummers should be on stage.)

Page 170: The performing drummer should use not a military (snare) drum, but a child's toy.

Page 218: NOTE: This chorus should consist of 12 sopranos and 12 altos. It is preferable to use the voices of choirboys. But if this is problematic, it is possible for these parts to be sung by 24 qualified voices from the opera chorus.

Page 267: End of Act I.

Page 268: NOTE: The artist performing the *Celesta* part should be a good pianist.

Page 294: The "Frullate" (flutter-tongue) is produced by pronouncing the letter *r*, preceded by a *t: trrrrrrr...* etc.

Page 451: If a *Celesta* is unavailable, its part may be performed on a piano.

THE NUTCRACKER

Complete Ballet in Full Score

THE NUTCRACKER

Peter Ilyitch Tchaikovsky

Op. 71 (1891–2)

OVERTURE.

УВЕРТЮРА. OUVERTURE.

pp
pp
pp
pp
pp
pp
Fl. I.
A
p
p
p
p
A
p
Fl. I.
Cl. I.
p
p
p
p
p
p

p
cresc.

B
mf
f
B

Picc.
cresc.
mf
f
sf

cantabile
grazioso
pizz.
Fl. I.
Ob. I.
Ob. II.
Cl. I.
Cl. II.
cresc.
cantabile
arco
C

grazioso
grazioso
arco

pp
cre - -
scen - -
do
ff
mp cre -
scen - do

pesante
pesante
pesante
pesante
pesante
pesante
pesante
pesante
pesante
pesante
pesante

D
p
D

mf
mp
p
pp

pp
p
pp
pp
pp
pp
pp
pp
pp
pp
pp
pp
pp
pp

E
Fl. I.
Cl. I.
p
Viol. II.
p
p
p
p
Viole.
p
p
E p
p
Fl. I.
p
Fl. II.
p
Ob. I.
p
Ob. II.
p
Cl. I.
p
Cl. II.
p
Viol. I.
p
p
p
p

p
cresc.
f
mf
p cresc.

Fl. I.
Fl. II.
Picc.
Ob. I.
Ob. II.
Cl. I.
Cl. II.
Fag. I.
Fag. II.
Triang.
V. I.
V. I.
cresc.
mf
f
F
sf
cantabile
grazioso
pizz.
p

Fl. I.
Fl. II.
cresc.
arco
pizz.
G
Ob. I.
Ob. II.
Cl. I.
Cl. II.
V. I.
grazioso
V. II.
Viole.

mp
f
ff
mf

H
pp
cre - -
scen - -
- do
ff
H

pesante
pesante
pesante
pesante
pesante
pesante
sempre ff
sempre ff
sempre ff
sempre ff
sempre ff
sempre ff
sempre ff
sempre ff
sempre ff
sempre ff
sempre ff
sempre ff
sempre ff
sempre ff
sempre ff
sempre ff
sempre ff
sempre ff

pizz.
pizz.
pizz.
pizz.
pizz.
pizz.

ACT I.
TABLEAU I.
SCENE.

СЦЕНА. №1. SCÈNE.

Cl.bas.
Fl. I.
Fl. II.
Cl. I.
Cl. bas.
Fag. I.
Fag. II.
Cor. I e II.
mp
p dolce
p
(Rideau)

Le président avec sa femme et ses invités ornent l'arbre de Noël.

The Judge, with his wife and guests, decorates the Christmas tree.

Cl. I.
Cl. II.
Fag. I.
Cor. III. IV.
p cresc.
mp cresc.
Fl. I.
Fl. II.
Cl. I.
Cl. II.
Cor. I. II.
Cor. III. IV.
cresc.

B

marcato

marcato

marcato

B

f
f
ff
ff
ff
f
f
f
f
f
f

Poco più sostenuto. (♩=116)
Fl. I.
Fl. II.
Ob.
Cl. I.
scherzando
Cl. II.
Fag. I.
scherzando
Fag. II.
Timp.
pizz.
pizz.
pizz.
Poco più sostenuto. (♩=116)
Fl. I.
scherzando
Fl. II.
Cl. I.
Fag. I.
pizz.

Fl. I.
Cl. I.
Fag. I.
Fl. I.
Fl. II.
Fl. III.
Ob.
Cor. ing.
Cl. I.
Cl. II.
Fag. I.
Cor. III. IV.
arco
arco
arco
arco
C
C

(Приготовить мал.фл.)
(Piccolo vorbereiten)
mf cresc.
poco cre - - - scen - - do
poco cresc.
mf
f

Fl.I.
Cl.I.
Fag. I.
pizz.
pizz.
pizz.
pizz.
Fl. I.
Fl.II.
Cl.I.
Fag.I.

string.
Fl.I.
Fl.II.
Cl.I.
Fag.I.
arco
string.
Tempo I. (𝅗𝅥 = 126)
Fl.I.
Fl.II.
Ob.
Cl.I.
Cl.II.
Fag.I.
Fag.II.
Timp. D.
arco
arco
arco
Tempo I. (𝅗𝅥 = 126)

D
D

Più moderato. (♩=108)
pp
mf
p
mp
poco cresc.
(Il sonne neuf heures. A chaque coup de l'horloge la chouette fait un mouvement avec ses ailes. Tout est prêt, il est temps d'appeler les enfants.)
Più moderato. (♩=108)

(The clock strikes nine. At each chime, the owl makes a movement with its wings. All is ready; it is time to call the children.)

Piccolo.
Мал.фл.
poco cresc.
cre - scen - do
cre - scen

un poco accelerando.
mf cresc.
mf cresc.
mf cresc.
mf cresc.
mf cresc.
mf cresc.
mf cresc.
mf
mf
mf
mf
mf
mf cre - - - - scen - - - do
mf cre - - - - scen - - do
mf cre - - - - scen - - do
mf cre - - - - scen - - do
do
un poco accelerando.

cresc.
cresc.
ff
sf

The door opens. Entrance of the children.

E
mf
cre
scen
do
f
sempre marcato
cresc.
mp
E

dim.
p
mf

F.

p *poco a poco cresc.*

Больш. Фл.
Gr. Fl.

mf *cresc.*

simile

poco a poco cresc.

F. *p* *poco a poco cresc.*

Les enfants s'arrêtent saisis d'étonnement.
Meno. (♩=100)
Meno. (♩=100)

The children stop, seized with astonishment.

Ob.
cresc.
mf
Arpa. (C, D, Es, Fis, G, A, B.)
mf
cresc.
cresc.
cresc.
cresc.
Ob.
G
cresc.
f
Arpa.
f
mf
cresc.
mf
cresc.
mf
cresc.
mf
cresc.
G

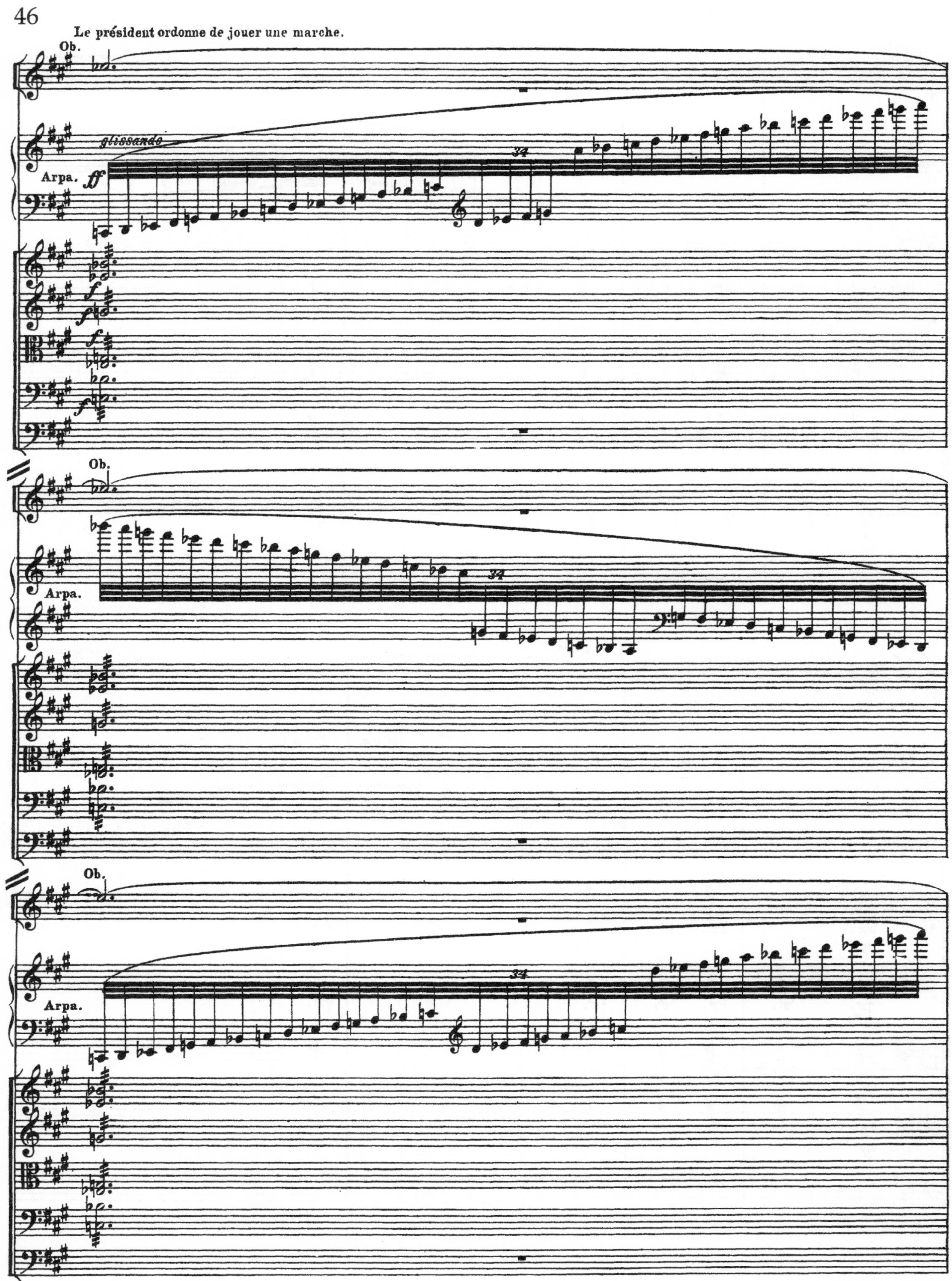

The Judge orders that a march be played.

Ob.
Arpa.
34
Ob.
Arpa.
34
sempre f
sempre f
Arpa.
34
pizz.
f
pizz.
f
pizz.
f
pizz.
f
pizz.
f

МАРШЪ. №2. MARCHE

(Б. Фл.)
(Gr. Fl.)
pizz.
pizz.
Палочкой.
Mit Paukenschlägel.

A.
p
mf
pp
pizz.
A.

B.
cre
scen
do
f
Палочкой.
Mit Paukenschlägel.
3
B.

pizz.
pizz.
arco
arco
arco

C.
C.

mf
p
pp
pizz.

D.
Палочкой.
Mit Paukenschl.
D.

pp
cre
scen
do
f
ff
Палочкой.
Mit Paukenschlägel.
pizz.
p

E.

mf

marcato

arco

E.

f
mf

F
marcato
marcato
F

3

mf
cresc.
pizz.

Палочкой.
Mit Paukenschl.
arco
arco

pizz.
pizz.

mf cresc.
mf cresc.
mf cresc.
cresc.
cresc.
cresc.
cresc.
cresc.
cresc.
Палочкой.
Mit Paukenschl.
cresc.
cresc.
cresc.
cresc.
cresc.

G
mf
f
3
pizz.
G

H
arco
arco
arco
H

ff
ff
ff
sf
f
sf
sf
f
sf
sf
f
sf
sf
f
sf
sf
f
sf
sf
f
sf
sf
f
sf
sf
f
sf
mf
mf
mf

mf
cresc.
mf
cresc.
mf
cresc.
mf
cresc.
mf
cresc.
mf
cresc.
cresc.
cresc.
cresc.
pizz.
mf
cresc.
pizz.
mf
cresc.

Палочкой.
Mit Paukenschl.
arco
arco

pizz.
pizz.

mf cresc.
f
ff
cresc.
Палочкой.
Mit Paukenschl.
arco

GALOP OF THE CHILDREN AND ENTRANCE OF THE PARENTS.

№3. ДѢТСКІЙ ГАЛОПЪ И ВХОДЪ РОДИТЕЛЕЙ.

№3. PETIT GALOP DES ENFANTS ET ENTRÉE DES PARENTS.

(Galop for the children.)

Cl. I.
Cl. II.
arco
Cl. I.
Cl. II.
arco

Cor. I. II.
p
p cresc.
Triang.
p
cresc.
p
cresc.
cresc.
p
pizz.
cresc.
p
pizz.
cresc.
p
Fl. I.
f
p
Fl. II.
f
p
Б. Фл.
Gr. Fl.
Fl. III.
f
p
Cl. I.
f
p
Cl. II.
f
p
Cor. I. II.
f
Triang.
f
mf
p
f
mf
f
mf
p
arco
f
mf
arco
f
mf

A
cresc.
cresc.
cresc..
ff
f
cresc..
cresc..
p cresc.
p cresc..
p
mf
p cresc..
mf
f
p
A

p
cresc.
mf
ff
p cre - scen - do
cresc.
cre - scen - do
cresc.

(Entrance of the parents, as "incroyables." [dandies, fops])

sf

B
pesante
pesante
pesante
pesante
pesante
pesante
pesante
pesante
unis.
pesante
pesante
div.
pesante
B

sf
sf
sf
sf
sf
sf
sf
sf
sf
sf
sf
sf
sf

Allegro. (♩.=120)
ff
in B.
in B.
sempre ff
sempre ff
f
f
f
mf
f
f
(muta in C.D.F.)
pizz.
f
pizz.
f
pizz.
f
pizz.
f
sempre ff
sempre ff
Allegro. (♩.=120)

Cor. I. II.
Cor. III. IV.
f
Cor. I. II.
Cor. III. IV.
Tromboni Ten.
Tr. Basso e Tuba.
p
arco
arco
arco
arco

C
in B
in B
Tamburino.
C

cresc.

D
Tamburino.
D

mf

mf
f
cresc.
cresc.
cresc.
cresc.
cresc.
cresc.

E
Tamburino.
E

СЦЕНА СЪ ТАНЦАМИ. №4. SCÈNE DANSANTE.

Arrivée du conseiller Drosselmayer. La grande horloge sonne, la chouette bat des ailes. Les enfants vont se blottir prés des parents; ils se rassurent en voyant que Drosselmayer porte des joujoux.

Andantino. (♩= 88.)

Flauto I.
Flauto II.
Flauto III. (Piccolo)
Oboi I. II.
Corno Inglese.
Clarinetto I in A.
Clarinetto II in A.
Clar. Basso in B.
Fagotto I.
Fagotto II.
Corni in F I. II. III. IV.
Trombe in A.
Tromboni Tenori.
Tr. Basso e Tuba.
Timpani. Fis, H, Cis,
Piatti, Tamburino e Triangolo
Violini I.
Violini II.
Viole.
Celli.
C-Bassi.

Andantino. (♩= 88.)

Arrival of Councillor Drosselmayer. The large clock chimes; the owl flaps its wings. The children go to cower by their parents; they are reassured by seeing that Drosselmayer carries toys.

Cor. I. II.
(закр. зв.)
(gestopft.)
Tromb. tenori.
Tromb. basso e Tuba.
marcatissimo
Ob.
espress.
Cor. I. II.
Cor. III. IV.
espress.
Tromb. tenori.
Tromb. basso e Tuba.

Stringendo.
Ob.
Cor. I. II.
poco cresc.
(закр. зв.)
(gestopft.)
Cor. III. IV.
Tromb.Tenori.
pesante
Tromb.Basso e Tuba.
pizz.
Stringendo.
Cor. I. II.
dim.
Allegro vivo. (♩ = 144.)
Cor. III. IV.
Trombe.
Tromb.Tenori.
Tromb.Basso e Tuba.
(открыто)
(Nicht gestopft.)
sempre pizz.
Allegro vivo. (♩ = 144.)

Fl. I.
A
mp
cresc.
Fl. II.
Fl. III.
Cor. I. II.
Cor. III. IV.
Trombe.
p
5
Fl. I.
Fl. II.
Fl. III.
f
Trombe.
Tromb. tenori.
Tromb. basso e Tuba.
mf
p
5

Fl. I.
mp
cresc.
Fl. II.
mp
cresc.
Fl. III.
mp
cresc.
Trombe.
Tromb. tenori.
Tromb. basso e Tuba.
p
p
p
B
Fl. I.
f
Fl. II.
f
Fl. III.
f
Ob.
p
Cl. I.
in A.
p
Cl. II.
in A.
p
p
mf
p
mf
p
mf
p
B mf
p

Ob. II.

Cl. I.

Cl. II.

Cor. I. II.

(открыто)
(Nicht gestopft.)

Cor. III. IV.

p

cre

Ob.

Cl. I.

Cl. II.

Cor. I. II.

Cor. III. IV.

scen - - do

f

Les deux enfants du Président attendent avec impatience la distrubition des cadeaux du parrain Drosselmayer. Celui-ci fait apporter deux caisses· de l'une il retire un grand chou de l'autre un grand pâté. Tout le monde est étonné.-

The two children of the Judge impatiently await the distribution of the gifts of godfather Drosselmayer. The latter has two boxes brought out: from one he withdraws a large cabbage and from the other a large meat pie. Everyone is astonished.

Più andante. (♩= 72.)
Ob.
Cor Ingl.
Cl. I.
Cl. II.
(Палочкой.)
(Mit Paukenschlügel.)
Piatti.
Più andante. (♩= 72.)
Ob.
Cor. Ingl.
Cl. I.
Cl. II.
Fag. I.
Fag. II.
Piatti.
Viole.
Celli.
Bassi.
C
p cresc. molto
mp molto cresc.
C

(Откр.)
(Nicht gestopft.)
(Откр.)
(Nicht gestopft.)
(non divisi)

Drosselmayer en souriant ordonne qu'on pose devant lui les deux cadeaux. Une grande poupée sort du chou et un soldat du pâté.

Drosselmayer, smiling, orders that the two gifts be placed in front of him. A large doll emerges from the cabbage and a soldier from the meat pie.

D

Fl. I.

p cresc. *f* *p poco cresc.*

Ob.

p poco cresc.

Corno ingl.

p cresc. *f*

Cl. I.

cresc. *f*

Cl. II.

cresc. *f*

Fag. I.

cresc. *f* *p poco cresc.*

Fag. II.

cresc. *f* *p poco cresc.*

Cor. I. II.

p poco cresc.

Viol. I.

p poco cresc.

Viol. II.

p poco cresc.

Viole.

p poco cresc.

Celli.

p poco cresc.

C. Bassi.

p poco cresc.

D

Fl. I.

mf *p poco cresc.*

Ob.

mf *p poco cresc.*

Fag. I.

mf *p poco cresc.*

Fag. II.

mf *p poco cresc.*

Cor. I. II.

mf *p poco cresc.*

mf *p poco cresc.*

mf *p poco cresc.*

mf *p poco cresc.*

mf *p poco cresc.*

mf *p poco cresc.*

Molto più presto.
mf
cresc.
ff
cres.
f
Molto più presto.

Pas de deux: The Ten Hours Leave.

f
ff
p
mf
arco
ff arco

F
ff
mf
p
pp
Triangolo.
pizz.
pizz.
F

sempre spiccato
sempre spiccato
p spiccato
p spiccato

poco cresc.
poco cresc.
poco cresc.
poco cresc.
poco cresc.
poco cresc.
poco cresc.
poco cresc.
poco cresc.
poco cresc.
poco cresc.

G
mf
p
pizz.
G

Presto. (♩=168)
Cl. I.
Cl. II.
Fag. I.
Fag. II.
Tr. Basso e Tuba.
arco
arco
arco
Presto. (♩=168)
Fag. I.
Fag. II.
Tr. Basso e Tuba
Timpani Fis, H, Cis.
H
pp ma un poco marcato
pp ma un poco marcato
H

cresc.
mf
p
sempre p

Tamburino.

ff
ff
ff
ff
ff
ff
ff
ff
ff
ff
ff
ff

cre - scen - do
mf cresc.
mf cresc.
p cresc.
p cresc.
mp cresc.
mf
cresc.
p cresc.
p
cresc.
cresc.
cresc.
cresc.
cresc.
cresc.
cresc.

K
K

СЦЕНА И ТАНЕЦЪ. №5. SCÈNE ET DANSE DU GROSS-VATER.

Claire et Fritz maintenant sont enchantés et veulent emporter les joujoux. Les parents le leur défendent. Claire pleure. Fritz fait le capricieux. Pour le consoler le vieux conseiller retire de sa poche un troisième cadeau: un casse-noisette. Claire est enchantée du petit bonhomme. Claire demande au conseiller la destination du cadeau; celui-ci prend une noisette et la fait casser par le casse-noisette. Fritz entendant le knak-knak du casse-noisette s'interesse à lui. Jl veut à son tour lui faire casser des noisettes. Claire ne veut pas le lui donner. Les parents font observer à la petite que le casse noisette ne lui appartient pas à elle seule. Claire cède son favori a son frère et regarde avec effroi comment Fritz lui fait casser deux noisettes, puis il lui fourre dans la bouche une si grande noix que les dents du casse-noisette se cassent.

Clara and Fritz are now enchanted, and want to carry the toys away. Their parents forbid them to do so. Clara cries. Fritz sulks. To console them, the old Councillor withdraws from his pocket a third gift: a nutcracker. Clara is enchanted with the little fellow. Clara asks the Councillor what the gift does; he takes a hazelnut and breaks it with the nutcracker. Fritz, hearing the crack-crack of the nutcracker, is interested. He wants to have a turn cracking nuts. Clara does not want to give it to him. Their parents point out to the young girl that the nutcracker does not belong to her alone. Clara yields her dear one to her brother, and watches in fear while Fritz breaks two hazelnuts and then puts in its mouth so large a nut that the nutcracker's teeth break.

Corno Ingl.
Fag. I.
Fag. II.
poco cresc.
sempre spiccato
mf
p
Corno Ingl.
Cl. I.
Fag. I.
mp

Corno Ingl.
Cl. I.
Fag.
A
dolce
p
mf
A
poco animando.
Fl. I.
Fl. II.
Ob.
Corno Ingl.
Cl. I.
Cl. II.
Fag. I.
Fag. II.
più f
arco
poco animando.

mf
f
più f

ritenuto
div.
dim.
ritenuto
dim.

B
Tempo I.
staccato
cresc.
p
pizz.
dolce
B
Tempo I.

molto riten.

mf

mf

mf

mf

mf

mf

pp

mf

mf

dim.

molto riten.

p

f

dim.

unis.

pp

mf

dim.

pp

mf

dim.

arco

mf

arco

mf

pp

dim.

Andantino. (♩=76)
poco accelerando
con grazia ed eleganza
cresc.
riten.
pizz
Andantino. (♩=76)
poco accelerando
Tempo I.
Трещётка. (Schnarre)
poco accelerando
cresc.
Tempo I.
poco accelerando
Più allegro. (♩=92)
Corno Ingl.
Трещ. (Schnarre)
arco
pizz.
Più allegro. (♩=92)

C
Fag. I.
mp
Fag. II.
mp
Cor. I II.
mp
Трещ.
Schn.
arco
mp
arco
mp
pizz.
mp
C
Fl. I. riten.
Tempo I.
poco acceler.
p
Fl. II.
p
Ob.
p
Cl. I.
p
Cl. II.
p
Fag. I.
Fag. II.
Cor. I II.
p
Cor. III. IV.
p
Трещ. riten.
Schn.
p
p
p
p
p
riten.
Tempo I.
poco acceler.

riten.
Più mosso. (𝅗𝅥=92)
poco accelerando
mf
cresc.
f
p
cresc.
mf
p cresc.
mf
p cresc.
mf
mf cresc.
f
mf cresc.
f
riten.
cre
scen
do
mf
p
f
mf
p
cre
scen
do
f
riten.
mf
mf
riten.
f
p
cre
scen
do
f
cresc.
f
p
cre
scen
do
f
cresc.
f
cresc.
mf
p
cre
scen
do
f
arco
mf
p
cre
scen
do
f poco acceler.
Più mosso. (𝅗𝅥=92)

a 2
ff
fff
f
cresc.
Tacet.

Fritz jette le jouet en riant. Claire le prend et avec des caresses tâche de consoler son favori. Elle enlève la poupée du lit et y pose le bonhomme.

Fritz throws the toy, laughing. Clara takes it, and tries to console her dear one with caresses. She removes the doll from the bed and lays the nutcracker there.

Andante. (♩= 72)
Ob.
Corno Ingl.
Cl. I.
Cl. II.
Fag. I.
Fag. II.
Viol. I.
Viol. II.
Celli.
Andante. (♩= 72)
D
Ob.
Cor. Ingl.
Cl. I.
Cl. II.
Fag. I.
Fag. I.
Cor. I. II.
dim.
pizz.
D

Lullaby. She is twice interrupted by Fritz and his friends, with their din of drums, trumpets, etc.

Fl. I.
Fl. II.
Fl. III
Ob.
Cl. I.
Cl. II.
Fag. I.
Fag. II.
Corni.
Trombe.
Tr. Tenori.
Tr. Basso e Tuba.
Più mosso. (♩=100)
Trompettes d'enfant.
Tambours d'enfant.
Fl. I.
Fl. III.
Ob.
Corni.
Trombe.
Tromboni e Tuba.
cresc.
Più mosso. (♩=100)

ПРИМѢЧАНІЕ. Кромѣ этихъ двухъ инструментовъ, дѣти, въ этомъ мѣстѣ, а также и въ слѣдующемъ, подобномъ же, могутъ производить шумъ и посредствомъ другихъ употребляемыхъ въ дѣтскихъ симфоніяхъ инструментовъ, какъ то: кукушки, перепела, тарелокъ и т. п. Только трещетка (Schnarre) здѣсь неумѣстна, ибо она уже находится въ оркестрѣ и предназначается для другой цѣли. Кукушка и перепелъ должны быть въ строѣ C-dur. *

Trombe.
Viol.I.
Viol.II.
Viole.
Tromp. d'enf.
Tamb. d'enf.
Ob.
Cor. Ingl.
Cl. I.
Cl. II.
Cl. Basso.
Fag. I.
Fag. II.
Corni.
Trombe.
Tromboni e Tuba.
Viol.I.
Viol.II.
Viole.
Più mosso. (♩=100)
Più mosso. (♩=100)

E
(Tacent.)
cresc.
cresc.
cresc.
cresc.
cresc.
cresc.
cresc.
cresc.
cresc.
cresc.
cresc.
cresc.
E

Pour couper court à ce tumulte, le Président prie ses invités de danser un Gross-Vater.

To cut short this tumult, the Judge invites his guests to dance a *Grossvater*.

F
mf
cresc.
ff
F

Tempo di Gross-Vater. (♩. = 69.)

Tempo di Gross-Vater. (♩. = 69.)

G
f
f
f
f
G

Примѣчаніе: Повторяется нѣсколько разъ *ad libitum.* *

SCENE.

СЦЕНА. № 6. SCÈNE.

Les invités remercient le Président et sa femme et s'en vont. On ordonne aux enfants d'aller se coucher. Claire demande la permission d'emporter avec elle le casse-noisette malade. Elle s'en va toute chagrine après avoir bien enveloppé son favori.

The guests thank the Judge and his wife, and leave. The children are ordered to go to bed. Clara requests permission to bring the sick nutcracker with her. She goes, very troubled, after having completely wrapped up her dear one.

mp
mp
mp
mp
mp
mp
poco più f
poco più f
poco più f
poco più f
poco più f
5
5

mf
3

A
dolce cantabile
arco
A

Cor. ingl.

poco più f

Cor. I. II.

Cor. ingl.

Cor. I. II.

Cor. III. IV.

più f

più f

più f

più f

più f

p

Cor. ingl.
ritenuto molto
a tempo
B
Cl. I.
Cl. II.
Cl. bas.
Fag.
Cor. I. II.
Cor. III. IV.
ritenuto molto
a tempo
Con sordini.
(sordini)
Con sordini.
Con sordini.
arco
ritenuto molto
a tempo
B
Cor. ingl.
Cl. I.
Cl. II.
Cl. B.
Fag.
pizz.
pizz.

La scène est vide. Il se fait nuit. La lune éclaire le salon par la fenêtre. Ciaire en toilette de nuit revient avec precaution; avant de s'endormir elle a voulu voir son malade chéri. Elle a peur; Elle s'avance vers le lit du casse-noisette qui lui semble produire une lumière fantastique. Minuit sonne. Elle regarde l'horloge et voit avec effroi que la chouette s'est transformée en Drosselmayer qui la regarde avec son rire moqueur. Elle veut s'enfuir, mais les forces lui manquent.

The stage is empty. Night has fallen. The moon lights the parlor through the window. Clara, in her nightclothes, returns cautiously; before going to sleep, she wants to see her cherished patient. She is afraid; she advances toward the bed of the nutcracker, who seems to be giving off a fantastical light. Midnight chimes. She looks at the clock and sees with fear that the owl has transformed into Drosselmayer, who looks at her with a mocking laugh. She wants to flee, but is unable.

Piccolo 1.
Piccolo 2.
(Tuba)
glissando

C
Pic. 1.
Pic. 2.
(Приготовить большую флейту)
(Grosse Fl. vorbereiten)
(Muta G, in Ges)
Con sordini.
cresc.
pizz.
C

Fl. I.
Pic. (Fl. II.)
Cor. ingl.
Cl. I.
Cor. I. II.
Cor. III. IV.
Arpa.
glissando
Viol. I.
Viol. II.
Viole.
Fl. I.
Piccolo. (Fl. II.)
Cor. ingl.
Cl. I.
Cor. I. II.
Cor. III. IV.
Arpa.
glissando
Viol. I.
Viol. I.
Viole.

(She is afraid.)

(Midnight chime.)

In the silence of the night, she hears the scratching of mice. She makes an effort to leave, but mice appear on all sides. She tries to flee, but is too afraid. She sinks into a chair. They all disappear.

Fl. I.
Picc. (Fl. II.)
Ob.
Cor. ingl.
Cl. I.
Cl. II.
Cl. Basso.
Fag.
Cor. I. II.
Tr. Basso e Tuba.
C. Basso.
cresc.
Senza sordini.
Fl. I.
Picc. (Fl. II.)
Tr. Ten.
Tr. Basso e Tuba.
Senza sordini.
Senza sordini.
Senza sordini.
Senza sordini.

F
Fl.I.
Picc. (Fl.II.)
(Приготовить большую флейту.)
(Grosse Fl. vorbereiten.)
Ob.
Cl.I.
Cl.II.
Tr. Ten.
Tr. Basso e Tuba.
poco cresc.
cresc.
F
Ob.
Cl.I.
Cl.II.
Cor. I.II. III.IV.
Tr. Ten.
Tr. Basso e Tuba.
Celli.
C. Bassi

cresc.
cresc.
cre - scen - do
cresc.
cresc.
cre - scen - do
cresc.
cresc.
cre - scen - do
cresc.
cre - scen - do
cre - scen - do

The Christmas tree grows, and gradually becomes enormous.

Ob.
Cl.I.
Fag.
Cor.I.II.
Cor.III.IV.
Viol.I.
Viol.II.
Celli.
G
poco a poco
cresc.
cre - scen - do
Fl.I.
Cor. ing.
Viole.
div.
arco.

cre - - - - - - scen - - - - - - - do

(Больш. фл.)
(Gr. Flöte)

cre - - - - scen - - - - do

(Больш. фл.)
(Gr. Flöte)

cre - - - scen - - - do

cre - - - - scen - - - - do

cre - - - - scen - - - - do

cresc.

cre - - - - scen - - - - do

cresc.

cre - - - - scen - - - -

cre - - - - scen - - - - do

cre - - - - scen - - - - do

cre - - - - scen - - - - do

sempre cre - - - - - - scen - - - -

cre - - - - scen - - - - do

cre - - - - scen - - - - do

cre - - - - scen - - - - do

pizz.

cre - - - - scen - - - - do

cre - - - - - - scen - - - -

do
do
Timp. A, E, F.
do
mf
f cresc.
ff
fff
arco
do

H
cre
scen
do
poco
a
poco
cresc.
espres.
unis.
H

sempre marcato

cresc.
fff
I

cre - scen - do
cresc. molto
poco a poco
cresc.
Platti
Gr. C.

marcatissimo
marcatissimo
marcatissimo
Cassa.
Tremolo.
cre
scen
do

scen
do
fff
cresc.
3

K
Piatti.
K

Gl.-Spiel.

P.

Gr.C.

L
f
f
f
fff
sfp
8
L

Atacca subito

СЦЕНА. № 7. SCÈNE.

Allegro vivo. (♩=144)

Примѣчаніе. *) Артистъ барабанщикъ долженъ бить не въ военный барабанъ Tamburo militare, а въ игрушечный, дѣтскій. *

The sentry cries "Who goes there?" No response. He fires a shot.

Gun shot.

Les poupées sont effarouchées. La sentinelle réveille les lapins à tambour.

2 Oboi.

Fag. I.

ff marcato

Cor. I.

p

p a punta d'arco

p a punta d'arco

p a punta d'arco

sf

Fl. I.

2 Oboi.

Cor. Ing.

Cl. I.

Cl. II.

Fag. I.

Fag. II.

Cor. I. II.

Cor. III. IV.

The dolls are startled. The sentry wakes the rabbit drummers.

The rabbits drum the alarm.
(The mice and the gingerbread soldiers prepare for battle.)

Piccolo.
Kl. Fl.
div.

The battle.

sempre ff
sempre ff
sempre ff
sempre f ma non troppo
sempre f ma non troppo

Tamb.d'enf.

ff
ff
fff
fff
fff
mf
ff
p
f
p
f
p
f
p
f
f
ff

B
fff
mf
ff
sempre ff
div.
B
sempre ff

sempre ff
sempre ff
cresc.
unis.

scen
do

Les souris triomphent et dévorent les soldats à pain d'épice.

The mice triumph, and devour the gingerbread soldiers.

Casse-noisette appelle sa vieille garde. Il crie: „aux armes!"

The nutcracker calls in his old guard. He cries: "To arms!"

Le roi des souris arrive. Son armée l'acclame.
C
a 2.
Imo
C

The Mouse King arrives. His army cheers him.

8 8 sempre sempre sempre ff ff ff sempre ff sempre ff sff sff sff sff fff fff a 2. f f

The second battle.

ff
sf
sempre
f ma non troppo
p
f

ff
ff
ff
ff
fff
fff
ff
ff
mf
f
f
f
p
f
p
f
p
ff

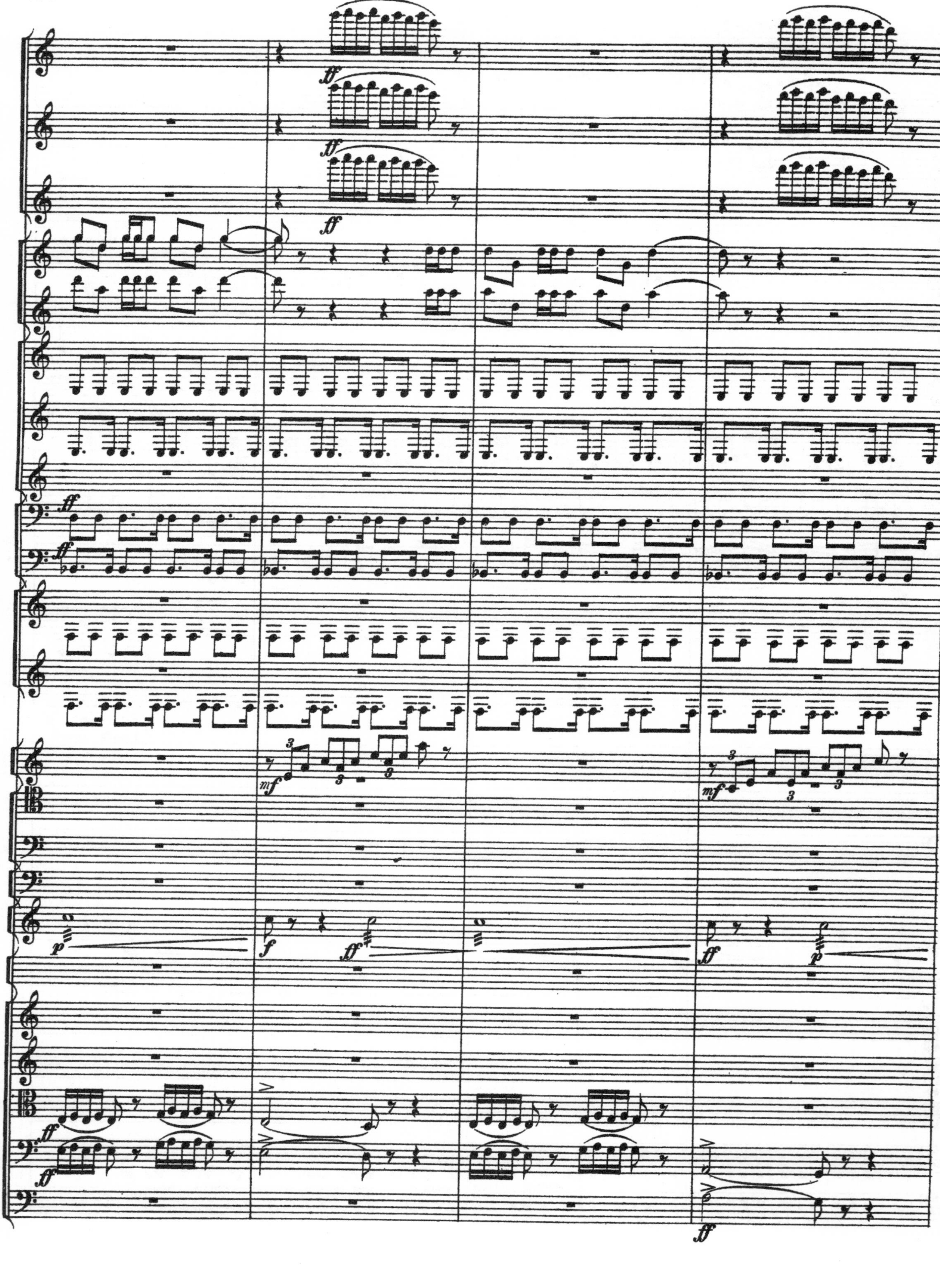

ff
ff
fff
fff
fff
f
mf
f
p
f
p
f
p
ff

fff
fff
fff
fff
fff
fff
fff
mf
cresc.
ff
ff
sempre
ff
sempre
ff
divisi.
sempre
ff

sempre
sempre
cre - - - - scen - - - -
unis.

do
ff

D
sempre fff
sempre fff
sempre fff
sempre fff
sempre fff
sempre fff
sempre fff
sempre fff
sempre fff
sempre fff
sempre fff
sempre fff
sempre ff
sempre ff
D

sempre fff
sempre fff
ff

Claire jette son soulier sur le roi des souris et tombe évanouie.

Clara throws her shoe at the Mouse King and falls into a faint.

Cl. I.
Cl. II.
Fag. I.
Fag. II.
fff
pizz.
Tromboni Tenori.
Trom. Basso e Tuba.
cre - scen - do
dim.

TABLEAU II.
SCENE.

СЦЕНА. №8. SCÈNE.

Une forêt de sapins en hiver. Les gnomes avec des flambeaux se placent prés de l'arbre de Noël pour faire honneur au prince, à Claire et aux joujoux qui vont se placer sur l'arbre.

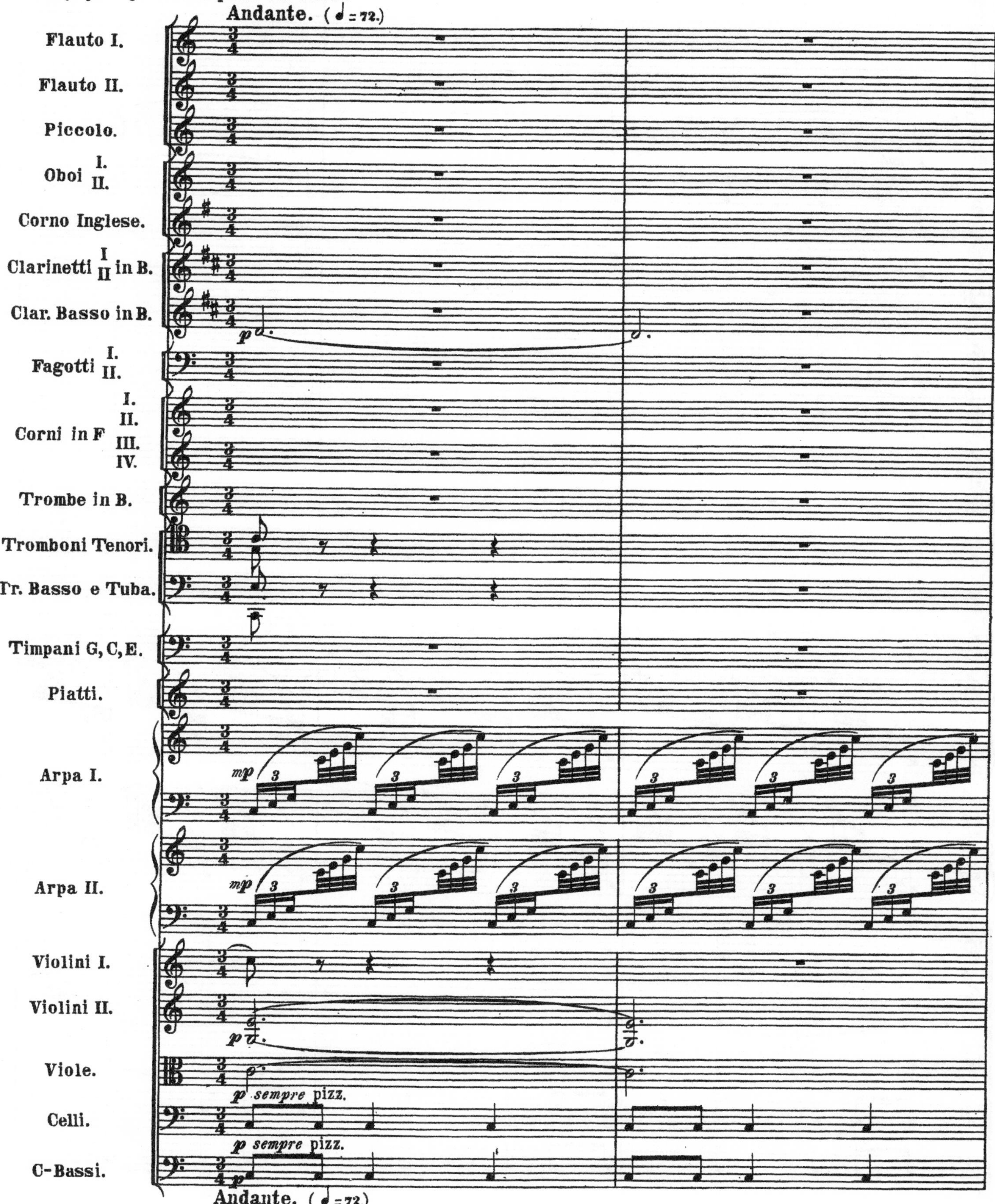

A forest of fir trees in winter. Gnomes with torches stand by the Christmas tree to honor the prince, Clara, and the toys that will be placed on the tree.

cantabile
p cantabile
p
p
cantabile
p cantabile
p
3
p
p
p

poco cresc.
poco cresc.
poco cresc.
mf
mf
poco cresc.
poco cresc.
mf
mf
poco cresc.
poco cresc.
poco cresc.
poco cresc.
poco cresc.
poco cresc.
poco cresc.

f
dim.
mp
f
dim.
mp
mf
mf
mf
mf
mf
p
p
p
p
p
p
p
p
p
p
p
p

cresc.
cresc.
cresc.
cresc.
cresc.
cresc.
cresc.
cresc.
cresc.
cresc.
cresc.
cresc.

3
f

A
Sul G
espr.
Sul G
espr.
divisi
espr.
A

cresc.
cresc.
cresc.
cresc.
cresc.
cresc.
cresc.
ff
ff
ff
ff
ff
ff
cre - - scen - - do
cre - - scen - - do
ff
ff
cresc.
cresc.
cresc.
cresc.
cresc.
ff
ff
ff

unis.
arco
arco

fff
fff
fff
fff
fff
fff
ff
ff
ff
largamente
largamente
div.
largamente
div.
largamente
largamente

B
fff
8
5
Timp.
Piatti
3
unis.
B

ff

C
a 2
marcatissimo
Piatti.
C

con tutta forza
sempre ff
fff
pp
f

(Muta E in D.)
pizz.
pizz.

mp
dim.
pizz.
mf
mp
3

D
p
cresc.
f
crescendo
D

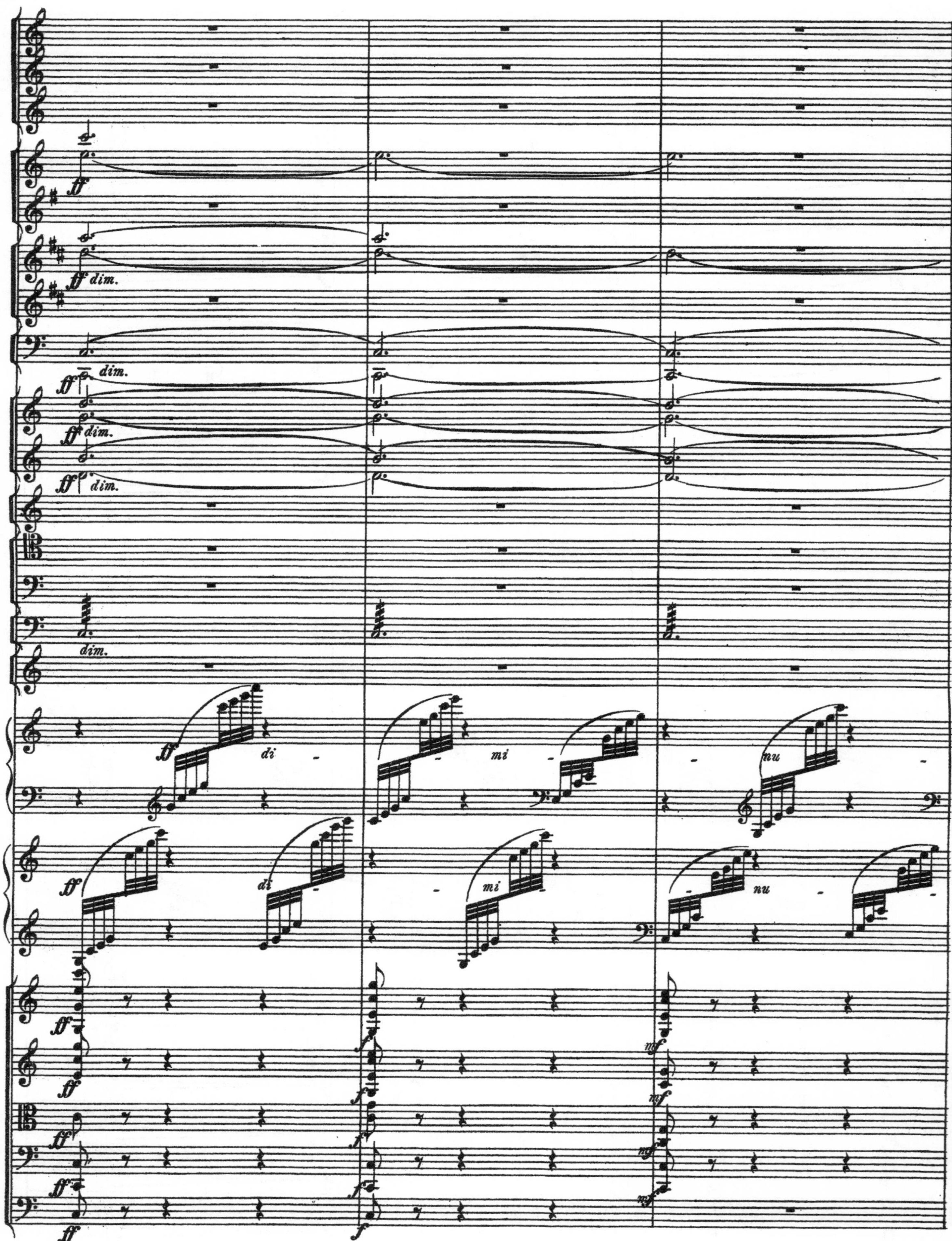
ff
ff dim.
dim.
ff dim.
ff dim.
dim.
ff
di
mi
nu
mf
f

en
do
en
do

ВАЛЬСЪ СНѢЖНЫХЪ ХЛОПЬЕВЪ. №9. VALSE DES FLOCONS DE NEIGE.

*) ПРИМѢЧ. Хоръ этотъ долженъ состоять изъ 12 сопрано и 12 альтовъ. Всего болѣе желательны голоса мальчиковъ изъ пѣвческаго хора. Но если это затруднительно, то можно поручить исполненіе этой хоровой партіи 24 наилучшимъ по качеству голоса хористамъ оперы. *

Fl. I. II.
Picc.
Cl. Basso.
Fag.
arco
poco cresc.
Fl. I. II.
Fl. I. II.
Cor. I. II.

A
Fl. I.II.
sempre a 2
mp
Arpa I.
mf
Arpa II.
mf
pp
pizz.
arco
pp
pizz.
pp
p
A
Fl. I. II.
f
mp
Arpa I.
mf
Arpa II.
mf
poco cresc.
poco cresc.
poco cresc.
poco cresc.
poco cresc.
pp
pp
pp
pp
pp

Fl. I. II.
2 Cl. in A.
Arpa I.
Arpa II.
B
a 2
poco cresc.
cresc.

Fl. II.
Cl. II.
cresc.
f
Fl. I. II.
mf
Cl. I. II.
Cl. Bas.
Fag.
a 2
Timp.
mp
Triang.
Arpa I.
Arpa II.
pizz.

Arpe I e II.

C
mf
espres.
Arpe I e II.
sempre pizz.
arco
C

mf
Arpe I e II.

Triang.
Arpe I e II.
arco
pizz.

sempre a 2
D
3
mf
Arpe I e II.
pizz.
8
D

cresc.
f
mf
p
sempre pizz.
pizz.
ff
Хоръ. За сценой.
A
13

Fl.
C. Ing.
Fag.
Хоръ.
а
Fl.
C. Ing.
Fag.
Хоръ.
а

E
mf
p
p
p
p
p
Glockenspiel.
mf
mf Arpa I Solo.
a – – – – – – – , a – – – – – – – –
pizz.
pizz.
p
p pizz.
p
p
p
E

poco cresc.
Triangolo.
a
a

Triangolo.

Arpe I e II.

arco

arco

arco

arco

divisi

pizz.

pizz.

pizz.

sempre pizz.

arco
pizz.
arco
divisi
sempre pizz.

F
a 2
p
a 2
p
p
a 2
p
p
p
Triang.
p
Arpa I.
p
Arpa II.
p
f
A
a
arco
divisi
p
pizz.
unis.
p sempre pizz.
F
p sempre pizz.

poco cresc.
mf
cresc.
ff

G
dim.
p
mf Jeu de cloches.
Glockenspiel.
glissando
mp
f
a
unis.
G

Arpe I e II.
a

poco cresc.
poco cresc.
poco cresc.
poco cresc.
poco cresc.
poco cresc.
poco cresc.
poco cresc.
A. I. II.
cresc.
cresc.
a
poco cresc.
poco cresc.
poco cresc.
poco cresc.
poco cresc.

A. I. II.

poco cresc.
poco cresc.
Muta D in E.
Triangolo.
p
poco cresc.
p
poco cresc.
pizz.
p
poco cresc.
sempre pizz.
p
poco cresc.
arco
p
poco cresc.

H
mf
cresc.
Arpa I.
Arpa II.
arco
pizz.
H

(G, C, E.)
poco
a
poco
Arpa I e II.
arco
arco

cresc.
ff
f
poco
a
poco
sff
p

a 2
cresc.
ff
a 2
sffp

poco a poco

8
ff
ff
ff
ff
cresc.
poco
a
poco

ff

sfp
sfp
sfp
sfp
fff
sff
Arpe I e II. (Ais, B, Cis, Des, E, Fes, G.)
sff
sff
sff
sff

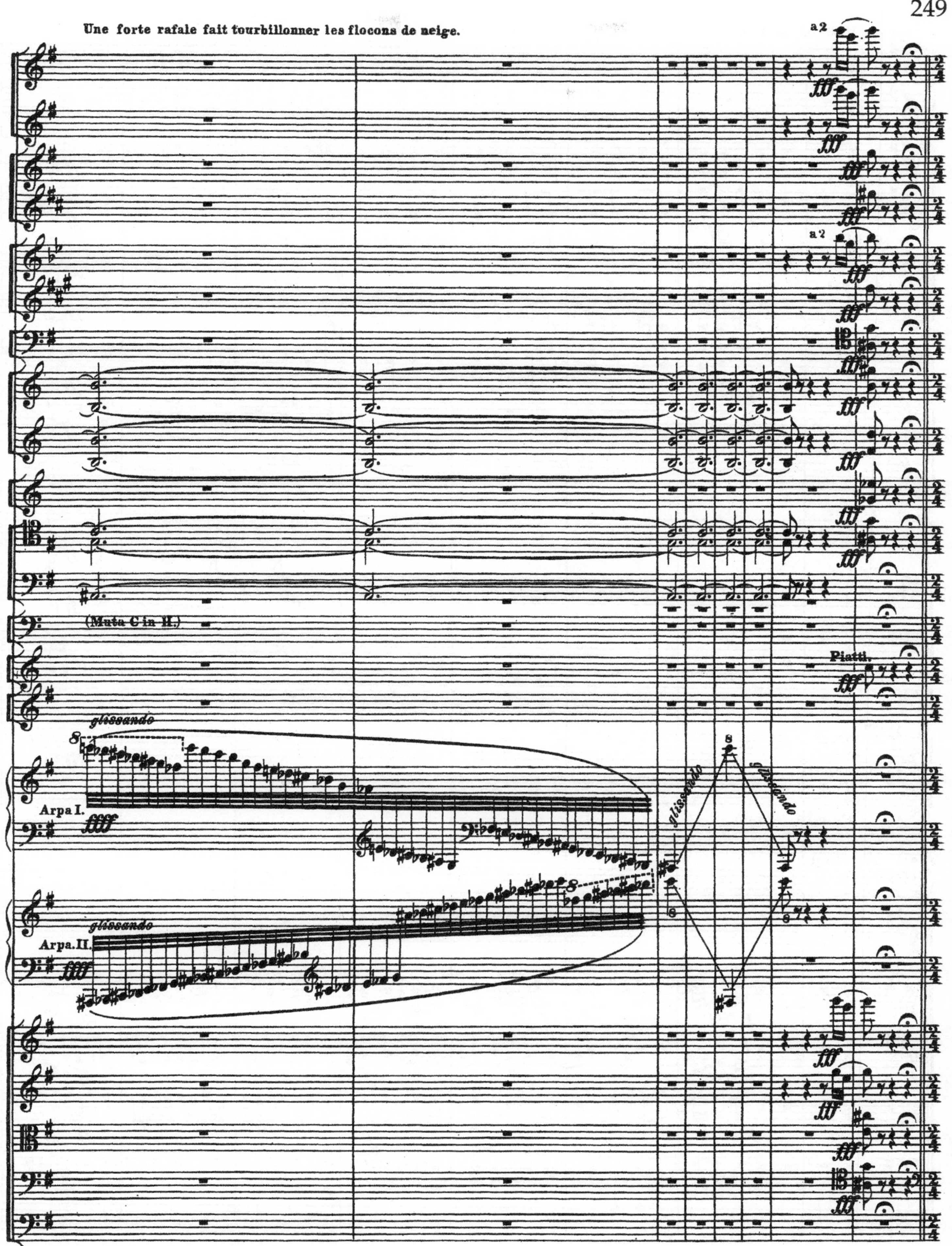

A strong gust whirls the snowflakes around.

Fl. I. e II.
Presto. (♩=168)
Pic.
Ob.
Cor. ingl.
Cl. I. II.
Cl. bas.
Fag.
Cor. I. II.
Cor. III. IV.
Trombe.
Tr. Ten.
Tr. Bas. e Tuba.
Timp.
Piatti.
Glock. spiel.
Presto. (♩=168)
Arpe I e II.
Хоръ.
Presto. (♩=168)
cresc.
p cresc.
pp
mf
ff
fff

fff
p cresc.
cresc.
f
ff
pp
mf
fff
p

K
fff
pp
Arpe I e II.
p
f
A
a
K

pp
- -, a - - - - - -, a - - a - - - ,
p

cresc.
f
ff
fff
mf

L
pp
cre
scen
do
ppp
L

a 2
mf cresc.
ff
pp
cre
scen
Piatti.
pp

a 2
mf cresc.
do
ff
Piatti.

Poco meno. (♩= 144)

Poco meno. (♩= 144)

Arpa I. gliss.
mf
Arpa II.
gliss.
8

M
pp
pp
Con sordini.
p
Arpa I. gliss.
Arpa II.
gliss.
Хоръ.
f
А
pp
pp
pp
M

8
Ar. I.
8
Ar. II.
8
a
a
pp
pizz.
pp
pizz.
pp

8

Ar. I.

8

Ar. II.

8

a

a

pp
pp
pp
pp
pp
pp
pp
Ar. I.
Ar. II.
cresc.
a
ff
a
pp
pp

pp
cresc.
mf
Ar. I.
Ar. II.
Arpe I e II a 2.
ff
a
arco

КОНЕЦЪ 1го ДѢЙСТВІЯ.*

ACT II.

SCENE.

СЦЕНА. № 10. SCÈNE.

Andante. (♩. = 60)

Flauto I.
Flauto II.
Piccolo.
2 Oboi.
Corno Inglese.
Clarinetto I in A.
Clarinetto II in A.
Clar. Basso in A.
Fagotti.
Corni in F I. II. III. IV.
Trombe in A.
Tromboni Tenori.
Tr. Basso e Tuba.
Timpani in E, H, G.
Piatti.
Celesta. (ou Piano) (oder Clavier.)
Arpe I e II.
Violino I.
Violino II.
Viole.
Celli.
C. Bassi.

mp

a 2.

f

ПРИМѢЧ. Артистъ, исполняющій партію *Celesta*, долженъ быть хорошимъ піанистомъ *
AVIS. L'artiste qui remplira cette partie devra être un bon pianiste.

Andante. (♩. = 60)

f

f

f

con anima

f

pizz.

mf pizz.

mf con anima

f

pizz.

mf

1.
2.

pesante
pesante
pesante
pesante

mf
mp
mp
mf
pesante
mp
mp
mf
pesante
mp
mp
mf
pesante
mp
mp
mf
pesante
mp
f
mf
mf
mf
f
mf

dim.
dim.
dim.
mf
dim.
mf
dim.
mf
dim.
mf
dim.
mf
mp
mf
mf
dim.
mf
dim.
mf
dim.
mf
dim.
dim.
arco
f
dim
arco
f
dim.
dim.
dim.

A
p
p
p
p
p cresc.
p
cresc.
p
f
mf
f
p
p cresc.
p
p
p
(Muta H in C.)
p
cre - - scen - - do
p
p
mp
mp
mp
mp
mp
A

ЗАНАВѢСЪ.
(Палочкой.)
(Mit Paukenschlägel.)
sempre ff
pizz.
arco

The enchanted palace of "Confiturembourg." [Kingdom of Sweets]

ff
f
sempre ff
8

5
8

B
ff
a 2
f
mf
sempre mf
sempre mf
sempre mf
Arpa I.
glissando
Arpa II.
glissando
7
B

A. I.
A. II.

A. I.
A. II.

1.
A. I.
A. II.

2.
poco cresc.
poco cresc.
poco cresc.
poco cresc.
poco cresc.
poco cresc.
A. I.
A. II.
divisi
unis.
arco
arco
poco cresc.
poco cresc.

Arpe I e II.
mp
mf
cresc.

ff
cresc.
f
mf
cresc.

ff cresc. ff cresc. ff cresc. cresc. cresc. cresc. cresc. ff cresc. ff cresc. f cresc. ff cresc. ff cresc. ff cresc. ff cresc. ff cresc.

(Приготовить большую флейту)
(Gr. Fl. vorbereiten)
Piatti.
(Просто)
(Wie gewöhnlich)

The Sugar-Plum Fairy appears with her attendants.

8
Celesta.
A. I.
A. II.
2 Viol. Soli.
Viol. I divisi.
2 Viole Soli.
pp
pp

D *dolcissimo*

Ob.

Cor. Ingl. *con dolcessa*

Cl. I.

Cl. II.

Cl. Basso.

Fag.

Corni I. II.

Timp.

Celli.

C-B.

D

Cor. Ingl.

Cl. I.

Cl. II.

Cl. B.

Fag.

Celli.

C-B.

СЦЕНА. № 11. SCENE.

Le fleuve d'essence de rose se gonfle. Claire et le prince paraissent.

Andante con moto. (♩ = 72)

Frullate *)

Flauto I.

Flauto II.

(Б. Фл.) (Gr. Fl.)

Flauto III.

2 Oboi.

Corno Inglese.

Clarinetto I in A.

Clarinetto II in A.

Clar. Basso in A.

Fagotti.

Corni in F I. II. III. IV.

Trombe in A.

Tromboni Tenori.

Tr. Basso e Tuba.

Timpani in G, C, E.

Celesta.

Arpa I.

Arpa II.

Violino I.

Violino II.

Viole.

Celli.

C. Bassi.

pizz.

Andante con moto. (♩ = 72)

*) Frullate исполняется посредствомъ растянутой буквы *p*, предшествуемой буквой *m*: *mppppppp*... и т. д. *

*) *Le Frullate se produit par la lettre* r *(devancée par* t*) prononcée d'une manière continue:* trrrrrrr... *etc.*

*) *Das Frullate wird durch den Buchstaben* r *(nach* t*) vorwärend gehalten gespielt, in dieser Weise:* trrrrrrr, *u. s. w.*

A river of rose oil swells. Clara and the prince appear.

poco cresc.

poco cresc.

poco cresc.

poco cresc.

poco cresc.

Celesta.

Arpa I.

Arpa II.

Celesta.
Arpa I.
Arpa II.

A

Celesta.

Arpa I.

Arpa II.

arco

un poco cresc.

A

Celesta.
A. I.
A. II.
un poco cresc.
un poco cresc.
poco cresc.

Celesta.
A. I.
A. II.

Un poco animando.
ff
9
ff
ff
Celesta.
8
A. I.
A. II.
Un poco animando.

B
Celesta
A.I.
A.II.
sempre f
sempre f
sempre f
sempre f
sempre f
B

(♩=80)
(просто)
fff
(просто)
fff
(просто)
fff
ff
ff
ff
ff
ff
ff
ff
ff
ff
ff
ff marcatissimo
ff
p
ff
8
8
8
ff
ff
ff pesante
(♩=80) ff pesante

C
Moderato. (♩. = 72)
Celesta.
A. I e II.
C
Moderato. (♩. = 72)

Douze petits pages arrivent portant des flambeaux.

Twelve little pages arrive carrying torches.

cresc.
Celesta.
A. I.
Arpe I e II.
a 2
cre - scen - do

D
(приготовить мал фл.)
(kl. Fl. vorbereiten.)
Celesta.
Arpa I.
Arpa II.
pizz.
dolce
pizz.
pizz.
dolce
pizz.
D

8
Celesta.
Arpa I.
Arpa II.

dolce
dolce
Celesta.
Arpa I. SOLA.
2 Viol. SOLI.
dolce

Celesta.
Arpa I.
2 V. S.

The nutcracker recounts his story, and how Clara saved him.

E
Poco più allegro. (♩=152)
Fl.I.
Fl.II.
Piccolo.
Ob.
Cor. ing.
Cl.I.
Cl.II.
Cl.bas.
Fag.
a 2
Corni.
Trombe.
Tromboni.
Timp.
E Poco più allegro. (♩=152)

cresc.
cresc.
cresc.
cre - scen - do
Gestopft.
Закр. зв.
Gestopft.
Закр.
cre - scen - do
cre - scen - do

cre - - scen - - do
Просто.
Nicht gest.
cre -
Просто.
Nicht gest.
cresc. poco a poco
Timp.
cresc. poco a poco
cresc. poco a poco
poco a poco cresc.
poco a poco cresc.

f
tr
cresc.
ff
a2
mf
cen
do
Просто.
Nicht gest.
Просто.
Nicht gest.
3

F
(Muta in B)
F

La cour célèbre le service rendu par Claire au prince.

Tempo precedente. (♩= 144)

The court celebrates Clara's service to the prince.

ff
mf
f

Sur un signe de la Fée Dragée une table resplendissante paraît.

Ob.
Cor. ing.
Cl.I.
Cl.II.
Cor. I.II.
Cor. III.IV.
pizz.

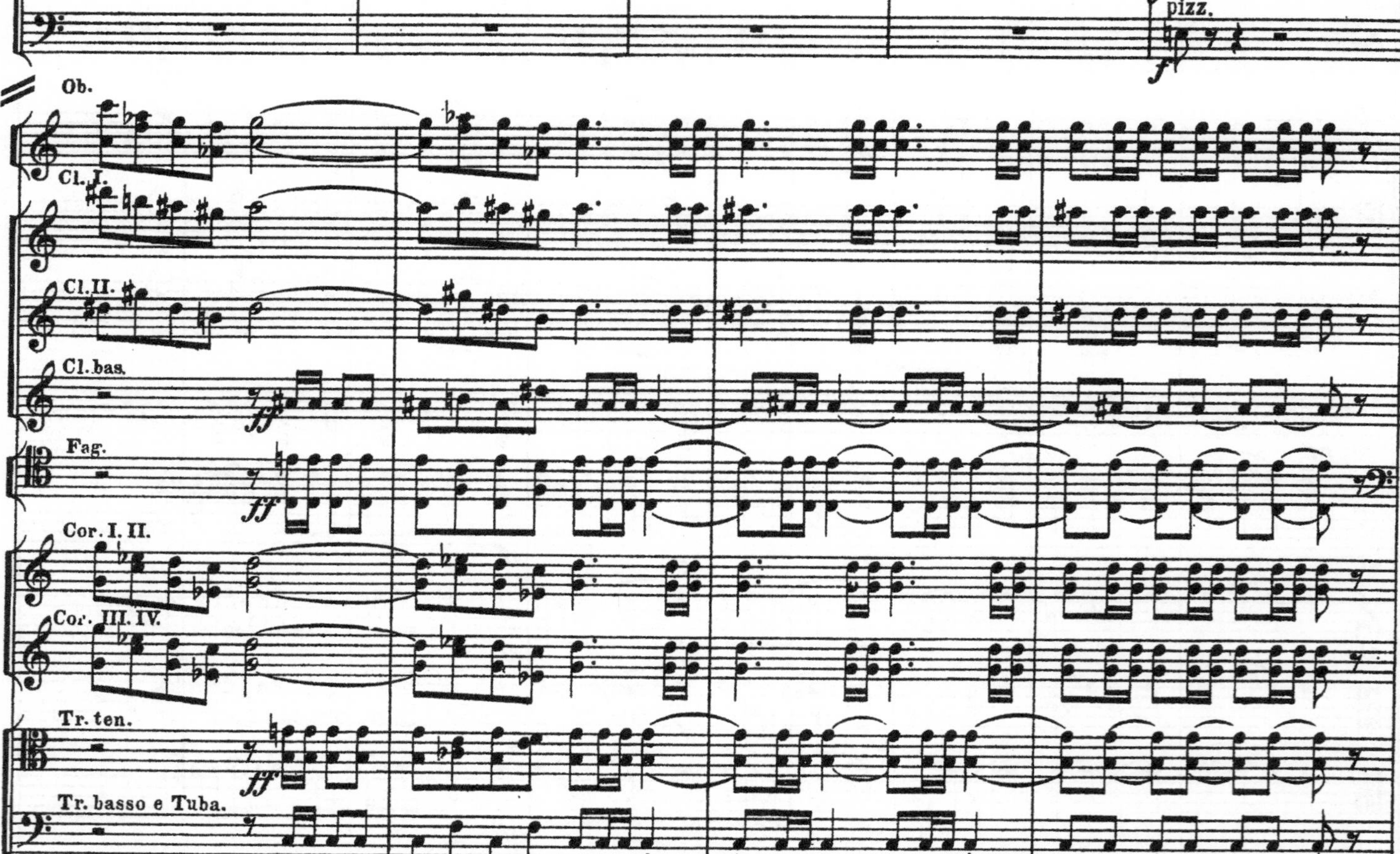

At a sign from the Sugar-Plum Fairy, a glittering table appears.

H
Ob.
Cor.ing.
Cl. I.
Cl. II.
Cl.bas.
Fag.
Cor. I. II.
Cor. III. IV.
Trombe.
Tr. ten.
Tr. basso e Tuba.
pizz.
cre - scen - do
ff
f
mf
p

ДИВЕРТИСМЕНТЪ. №12 DIVERTISSEMENT.

a) Шоколадъ. a) Chocolate. a) Le chocolat.

Cl.I.
Corni.
Trombe.
mf

Cl.I.
cresc.
ff
Cl. bas.
mf
Corni.
Trombe.
f
mf

a 2
div.
spiccato
spiccato
spiccato
pizz.
pizz.

f
f
f
f
f
f
p
p
p
p

Oboi
p
mf
Cor. Ingl.
p
mf
2 Tromboni ten.
pp
poco cresc.
Castagn.
p
cre
scen
do
con grazia
poco cresc.
con grazia
poco cresc.
arco
p
poco cresc.
arco
p
poco cresc.
Oboi.
f
Cor. Ingl.
f
2 Tromboni ten.
mp
cresc.
Castagn.
f cresc.
mf
cresc.
mf
cresc.
mf
cresc.
mf
cresc.

a 2
div.
div.
div.

ff
ff

Più mosso.
ff
unis.
unis.
unis.
f
f
f
f
arco
f
Più mosso.

ff
f
mp
mf
a 2
Sordini
Sordini
Sordini
Sordini
Sordini

b) Кофе. b) Coffee. b) Le café.

Cor. Ing.
Cl. I.
Cl. II.
Viol. I.
Con sordini.
molto espress.
Viol. II.
Con sordini.
molto espress.
Viole.
Celli.
Cl. I.
Cl. II.
Tamburino.
(Пальцемъ по кожѣ)
(Mit dem Daumen)
pp
Viol. I.
più f
Viol. II.
più f
Viole.
Celli.
A
Cl. I.
Cl. II.
Viol. I.
pp
cresc.
mp
Viol. II.
pp
cresc.
mp
Viole.
Celli.
A

Cor. Ingl.
Cl. I.
Cl. II.
Fag. I.
Fag. II.
Tamb.
Viol. I.
Viol. II.
Viole.
Celli.

B

Cor. Ingl.
Fag. I.
Fag. II.
Tamb.
Viol. I.
Viol. II.
Viole.
Celli.

B

Fag. I.
dim.
mf
p
Fag. II.
dim.
Viol. I.
poco cresc.
Viol. II.
Viole.
Celli.
Tamb.
pp
Cor. Ing.
Cl. I.
Cl. II.
Bassi
div.
Con sordini

Ob. I.

Cl. I.

Cl. I.

Viol. I.

Viol. II.

Viole.

Celli.

Bassi.

Fl. I.

D

Fl. II.

Fl. III.

Ob. I.

Ob. I.

Cor. Ingl.

Cl. I.

Cl. II.

Cl. Basso.

Viol. I.

Viol. II.

Viole.

Celli.

Bassi.

D

Fl.III.
(Приготовить мал. Фл.)
(Kl. Fl. vorbereiten)
Ob.I.
C.Ingl.
Cl.I.
Cl.II.
Cl.B.
Fag.I.
Fag.II.
Tamb.
Viol.I.
Viol.II.
Viole.
Celli.
Bassi.
morendo

c) Чай. c) Tea. c) Le Thé.

Fl. I.
Fag. I.
Fag. II.
sempre pizz.
sempre pizz.
sempre pizz.
sempre pizz.
Fl. I.
Picc.
Fag. I.
Fag. II.

Fl. I.
Picc.
Fag. I.
Fag. II.
A
A
Fl. I.
Picc.
Cl. I.
Cl. II.
Cl. Basso in B.
Fag. I.
Fag. II.
sempre mf
sempre mf
Cor. II.
Glock. jeu de cl.

mf
mf
mf
mf

cresc.
ff
(Приготовить больш. Фл.)
(Gr. Fl. vorbereiten.)

d) Трепакъ. d) Trepak. d) Trépak.

A
mf
sf
ff
f
p
A

B
a2
B

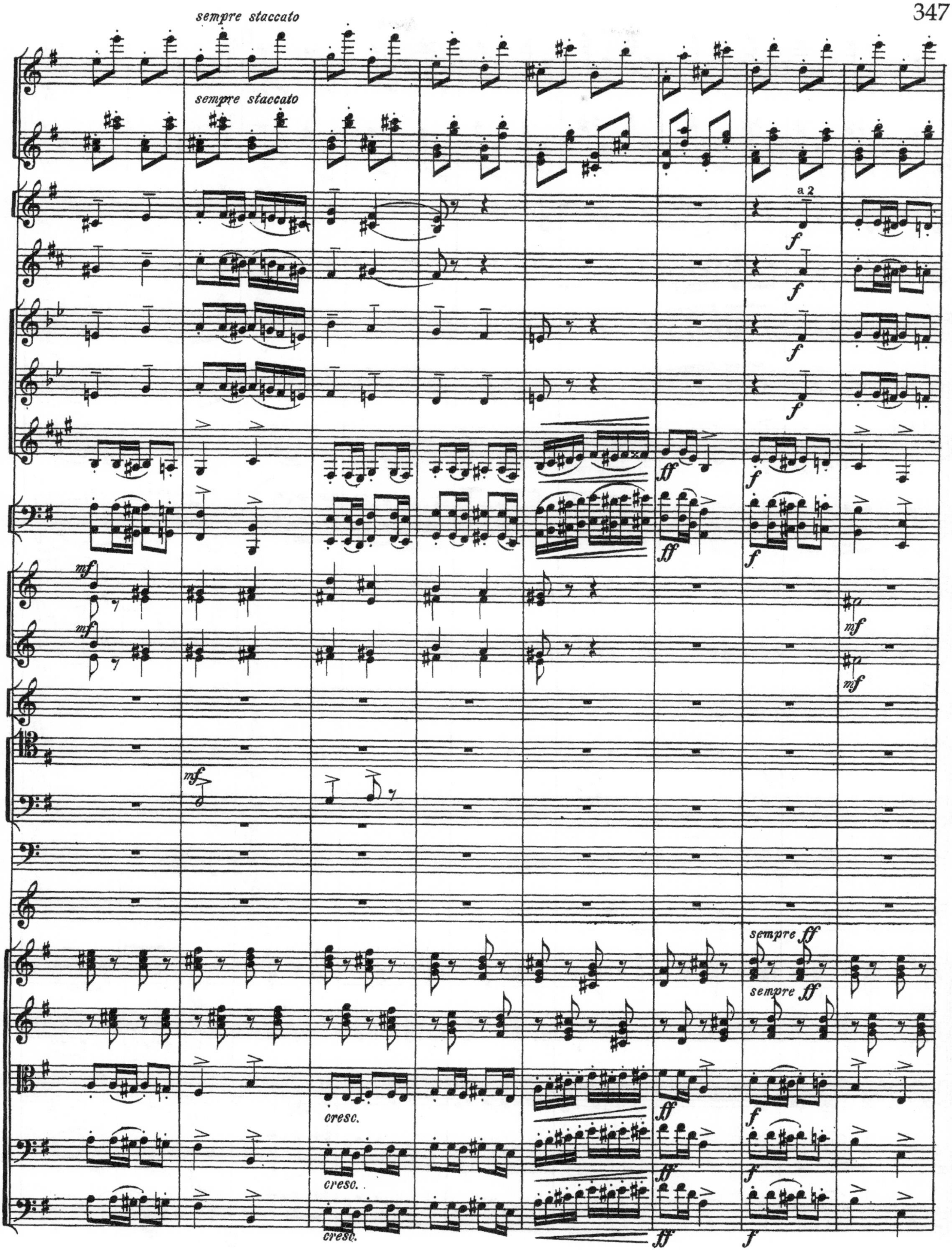

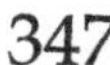

sempre staccato
sempre staccato
a 2
f
f
f
f
ff
ff
f
f
mf
mf
mf
mf
mf
sempre ff
sempre ff
cresc.
ff
f
ff
f
cresc.
cresc.
ff
f

C
mf
f
ff
C

ff
sf

Stringendo. *sempre fff*

sempre fff

sempre fff

sempre fff

sempre fff

sempre fff

sempre fff

sempre fff

sempre fff

sempre fff

sempre fff

fff

fff

sempre fff

sempre fff

sempre fff

sempre fff

sempre fff

sempre fff

sempre fff

Stringendo. *sempre fff*

Prestissimo.
Prestissimo.

e) Танецъ пастушковъ. e) Dance of the Mirlitons. * e) Les Mirlitons

* The Russian title is "Dance of the Shepherdesses." In performance, the shepherdesses play on mirlitons, early reed-flutes similar to kazoos. – Ed.

Fl. I. II.
p
cresc.
Fl. III.
p
cresc.
f
mf
Fag. I.
pp
mf
arco
mf
arco
mf
poco cresc.
poco cresc.
poco cresc.
mf
p
sf
mf
cresc.
A
ff
Cor. Ing. espress.
Cl. Basso.

Fl.I.II.
Fl.III.
pizz.
arco
sempre
poco più f
Cor.I.II.
cresc.
B

sf
mf
p cresc.
f
C
p
pp
pizz.
poco più f
cresc.

p
p
p
p
p
arco
p
arco
p
divisi
arco
p
arco
p
arco
p

D
div.
div.
sempre spiccato
sempre spiccato
sempre spiccato
D

p
mf
p
mf
pizz.
p
arco
p
poco più f
pizz.
p
arco
p
poco più f
unis. pizz.
p
arco
p
poco più f
pizz.
p
sempre pizz.
p
pizz.
p
sempre pizz.
p

E
sf
mf
p
cresc.
f
mf
p
cresc.
mf
E

mf
sf
p cresc.
f
poco più f
p
cresc.
pizz.

f) Mother Gigogne and the Clowns.*

f) **Полишинели.** f) **La mère Gigogne et les polichinelles.**

* "La mère Gigogne" is the French equivalent of the English "old woman who lived in a shoe," or any woman with many children. In English-language versions of The Nutcracker, this character's name is traditionally given as "Mother Ginger." – Ed.

A
a 2
unis.
A

(Б. Фл.)
(Gr. Fl.)
ff
staccato
staccato
pizz.
(non divisi)
pizz.
(non divisi)
divise
divisi a 3

unis.
unis.
div.

B

ff

ff

ff

ff

B

pesante
pesante
pesante
mf
sf
p

C
cresc.
sf
ff
f
pizz.
cre
scen
do
fff
C

ff
arco
f
arco
f
arco
f
arco
f

Tromb.
Triang.
pizz.

Allegro vivo. (♩= 144)

D

f

cresc.

ff

divisi
arco

Allegro vivo. (♩= 144)

D

pesante
pesante
sempre
sempre
pesante
pesante
unis
sempre

Poco più. (𝅗𝅥 = 160)
fff
Poco più. (𝅗𝅥 = 160)

E

mf *cresc.* *fff*

E

mf
cresc.
fff

8

WALTZ OF THE FLOWERS.

ВАЛЬСЪ ЦВѢТОВЪ. №13. VALSE DES FLEURS.

Ob. I. II.
Cl. I. II.
Fag. I. II.
Corni I. II.
Corni III. IV.
Timp.
Arpa
f
mf
dim.
p
ff
cadenza ad libitum

Arpa
Arpa
riten.
a tempo
Corni I. II.
dolce cantabile
p
Corni III. IV.
p dolce cantabile
Viola.
pp
simile
Cello.
simile
pp
Basso. pizz.
p a tempo
Cl. I. II. SOLO I°
cre - scen - do
p
mf
Viol. I.
pp
mp
Viol. II.
po - co cresc.
pp
mp
pp
Viola.
f po - co cresc.
mp
pp
Cello.
po - co cresc.
mp
pp
Basso.
po - co cresc.
mp
pp

Cl. I. II.
A
Cor. I. II.
Cor. III. IV.
Viol. I.
Viol. II.
Viola.
pp
simile
Cello.
Basso.
cre - scen -
cre
Cl. I. II.
Viol. I.
Viol. II.
Viola.
Cello.
Basso.
scen - do -
f
mf
arco

B
ff
ff
ff
ff
ff
mf
mf
mp
f
B

1.
2.
mf
sf
ff
f

Fl.I.
Fl.II.
Cl.I.II.
a 2
Cor.I.II. cantabile
Cor.III.IV.
Viol.II. cantabile
Viola.
simile
Cello.
simile
Basso. pizz.
Fl.I.
Fl.II.
Cl.I.II.
cresc.
dim
dim.
Cor.III.IV.
Viol.I.
Viol.II.
simile
Viola.
Cello. poco cresc.
Basso.
poco cresc.

Fl. I.
Fl. II.
Cl. I. II.
Cor. I. II.
Cor. III. IV.
Viol. I.
Viol. II.
Viola.
Cello.
Basso.
C
mp cresc.
cresc.
cre - scen - do
arco

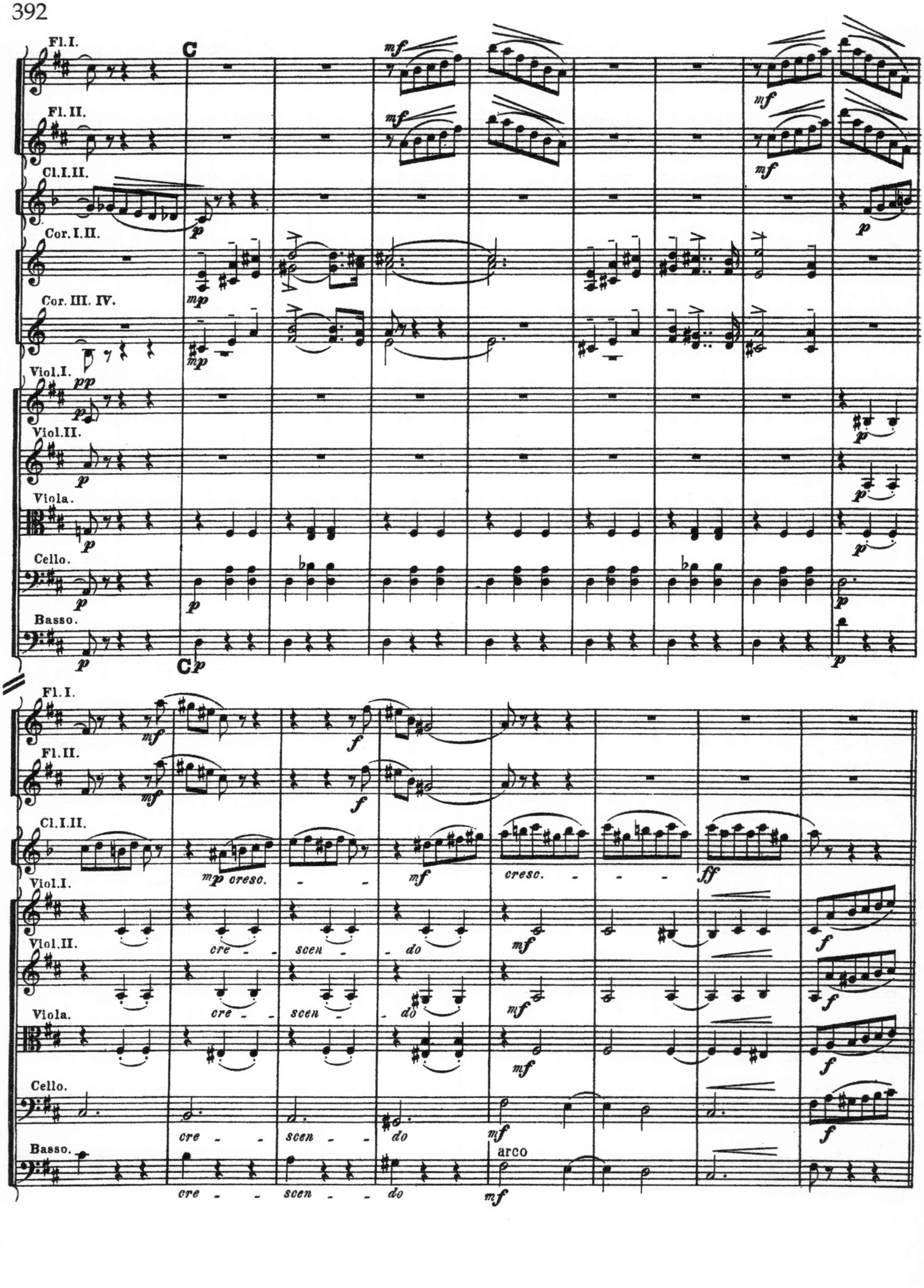

D
ff
mf
mp
f

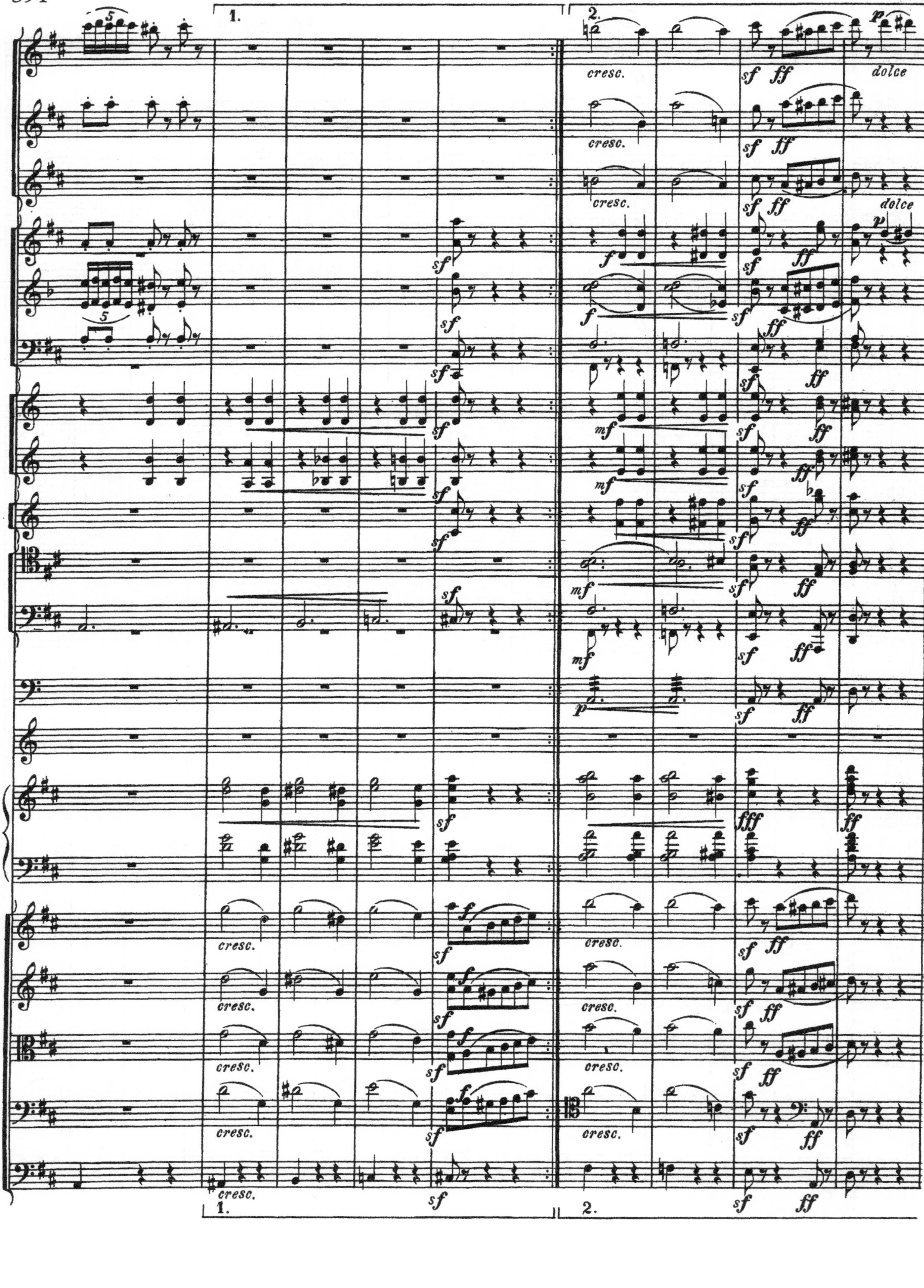
1.
2.
cresc.
dolce
sf
ff
mf
fff
p

Fl. I.
Ob. I. II.
Cl. I. II.
Fag. I. II.
Viol. I. 2 Viol. I Soli.
Viol. II. 2 Viol. II Soli.
Viole. 2 Viole Sole.
Bassi. 2 Bassi Soli.
Fl. I.
Ob. I. II.
Cl. I. II.
Fag. I. II.
Cor. I. II.
Viol. I.
Viol. II.
Viola.
Basso.

pp
pp
p
p
p
p
E

pp
mf
TUTTI
mp
con anima
f
arco TUTTI

Ob.I.II.
Cl.I.II.
Fag. I.II.
Cor.I.II.
Cor.III.IV.
Tromb.
mf
p
Ob.I.II.
Cl.I.II.
Fag.I.II.
Cor.I.II.
Cor.III.IV.

F
Ob. I. II.
mf
Cl. I. II.
mf
Fag. I. II.
mf
Cor. I. II.
mf
Cor. III. IV.
mf
Tromb.
mf
mf
mf
f
f
mf
p
p
p
p
p
p
mf
mf
F
Ob. I. II.
cresc.
f
Cl. I. II.
cresc.
f
Fag. I. II.
cresc.
f
Cor. I. II.
cresc.
Cor. III. IV.
cresc.
cre - scen - do
f
cre - scen - do
f
ff
ff
ff
dim.
ff
ff
ff
dim.
cre - scen - do
f

G
p
p
p
p
p
p
p
p
dolce
p
dolce
p
pizz.
p
pizz.
p
pizz.
G p

cresc.
cresc.
cresc.
p cresc.
a 2 cresc.
p
cre - scen - do
f
pp
arco
mf

H
ff
mf
a 2
f
pp
cantabile
H

mf mf a 2 mf f cre - scen - mp cre - scen - cre - scen - do cresc. mf f cresc. mf f cre - scen - do mf mf cre - scen - do mf cre - scen - do

I
a 2
do
cresc.
I

mf
mf
a 2
f
mf
mp
cre
scen
cresc.
mf
p
mf
mf
cre
scen
do
f
mf
cre
scen
do
f
mf
cre
scen
do
mf
mf
cre
scen
do

do
f
mf
ff
mp
5

1.
sf
f
cresc.
1.

2.
f cresc.
f cresc.
f cresc.
sf
ff
mf
p
cresc.
cresc.
cresc.
cresc.
sff
fff
2.

dolce
dolce
a 2
dolce
Muta D in C.

p
pp poco
a
poco
cresc.
mf
cresc.
pp
mf cresc.

a 2
Timp A.C.E.

Muta C in D.

ff
p
cre
scen
do
f

Timp. A. D. E.

L
ff
p
cre
f
L

scen
do
fff
f

Fine.

№ 14. PAS DE DEUX.

Arpa I.
Arpa II.
ff
f
mf
Arpa I.
Arpa II.
ff
divisi.

Arpa I.
cresc.
Arpa II.
cresc.
mf
A
Arpa I.
f
mf
Arpa II.
f
mf
f
f
mf
f
mf
ff
mf
f
A
mf

ff

ff

ff

ff

a2

ff

a2

ff

cresc.

cresc.

cre - - scen - - do

cre scen do

cre - - scen - - do

cre - - scen - - do

cre - - scen - - do

Arpe I e II.
arco
dim.
unis.
unis.

Arpe I e II.
div.

Arpe I e II.

B
mf
dim.
diminuendo
Arpe I e II.
f
unis.
B

Poco stringendo.
Poco più mosso. (𝅗𝅥=76)
p
dolce cantabile
Arpe I e II.
arco
pp
Poco stringendo.
Poco più mosso. (𝅗𝅥=76)

Ob.
Cl. Basso.
dolce
Cor. I.II.
Cor. III.IV.
SOLA.
p
Arpa I.
SOLA.
mp
Arpa II.
arco
p
Cl. Basso.
cantabile
Cor. I.II.
sempre p
Cor. III.IV.
sempre p
p
mp
Arpa I.
pp
pp
p
p
pizz.
p
pizz.
p
arco

Incalzando.

Tuba.

pp

p

mp

14

6

espr.

arco

Incalzando.

p
cre - - scen -
divisi
mp
mf
pp poco a poco
cre - - scen - do

Animando.

C

mp cre - scen - do

mp cre - scen - do

scen - do

cresc.

Animando.

C

Ritenuto
ff
ff
ff
ff
ff
f
f
f
ff
ff
ff
ff
Ritenuto

Tempo I.
ff marcato
ff
f
pp
Tempo I.

a 2
pp
f

D
Poco stringendo.
cre - scen - do
pp poco cresc.
mf
Poco stringendo.
D

- scen - - do

- -do

- -do

- -do

- -do

- -do

Tempo I.
Piatti.
Tempo I.

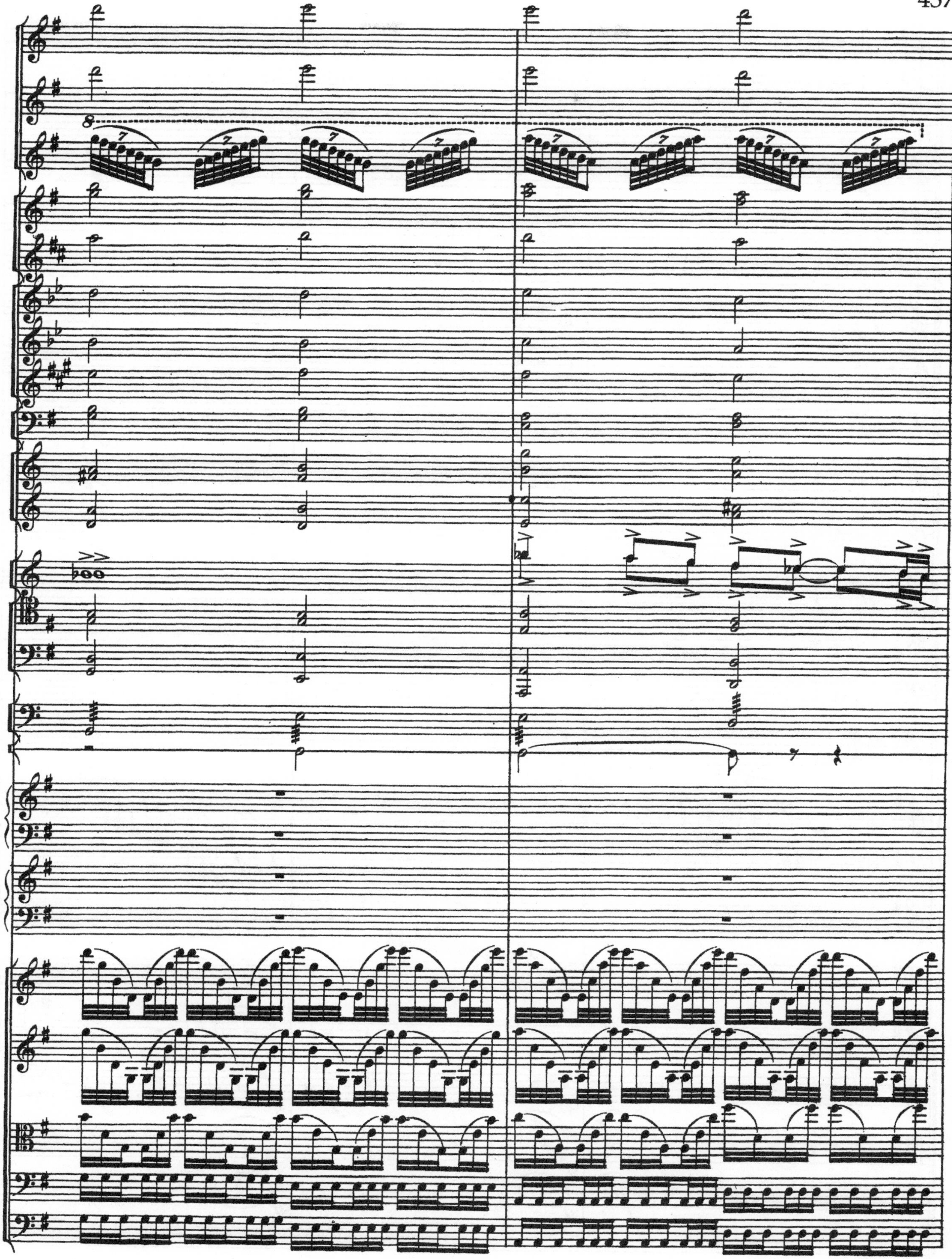

f
sf
ff
mf
9
10

10
10
10

E
ff
3
ff
3
3
E

mf
cresc.
fff
f
p
mp
ff

Trombe.
Tr. Ten.
Tr. Basso e Tuba.
A. I.
A. II.
Viol. I.
V. II.
Fl. I.
Cl. I.
Corni.
Tromb.
Tr. Ten.
Tr. Basso e Tuba.
A. I.
A. II.
Viol. I.
V. II.
Viole.

f
f
tr
tr
tr
pizz.
ff
pizz.
ff

f
f
f
f
tr
tr
tr

arco
arco

Var. I. (Pour le danseur)
Tempo di Tarantella. (♩.=168)
Flauto I.
Flauto II.
Piccolo.
2 Oboi.
Corno Inglese.
Clarinetto I in A.
Clarinetto II in A.
Clar. Basso in A.
Fagotti.
I.
II.
Corni in F
III.
IV.
Trombe in A.
Tromboni Tenori.
Tr. Basso e Tuba.
Timpani in H,A,D.
Tamburino.
Violino I.
Violino II.
Viole.
Celli.
C. Bassi.
mf
Tempo di Tarantella. (♩.=168)

Fl.I.
Fl.II.
Cor. Ingl.
Cl.I.
Cl.II.
Fag.

mf
mf

Fl.I.
Fl.II.
Cor. Ingl.
Cl.I.
Cl.II.
Fag.
Corni I.II.

A

p
p
p
p
p
p

A

p
mf
cresc.
Piccolo
piu f
cre - scen_do

B
a 2
Tambur.
pizz.
pizz.
pizz.
pizz.
pizz.
B

(Muta H in B)
arco
arco
arco
arco
arco

Danse de la Fée-Dragée.

Var. II. (Pour la danseuse).

mf
fp
p
pp
f
mf
p
p
p
p
p

A
div.
arco
arco
arco
arco
A

sf
mf
p
pp
arco.

sf
p
mf
cresc.
f
ff
pp

Celesta.
Fl. I.
Fl. II.
Fl. III.
Fag. I.
Fag. II.
Celesta.
Viol. I.
Viol. II.
Viola.
Cello.
B
a punto d'arco
a punto d'arco
a punto d'arco
Cl. I.
Celesta
cresc.
Viol. I.
Viol. II.
Viola.
Cello.
C-Basso.
C

divis.
pizz.
divis.
pizz.
divis.
pizz.
pizz.

Presto. (𝅗𝅥 = 184)
p
p
p
p
p
p
p
p
8
ff
pizz.
p
sempre pizz.
p
sempre pizz.
p
pizz.
p
pizz.
p
Presto. (𝅗𝅥 = 184)

D
p
D

sempre p
sempre p
sempre p
sempre p
sempre p

(Приготовить мал.Фл.)
(Kl. Fl. vorbereiten.)

Coda.

Vivace assai. (♩=168)
Flauto I.
Flauto II.
Flauto III. (Piccolo)
2 Oboi.
Corno Inglese.
Clarinetto I in A.
Clarinetto II in A.
Clar. Basso in A.
2 Fagotti.
Corni in F. I. II.
III. IV.
Trombe in A.
Tromboni Tenori.
Tr. Basso e Tuba.
Timpani in A. B. D.
Piatti e Gr. Cassa.
Violino I.
Violino II.
Viole.
Cello.
C-Basso.
arco
div.
p
Vivace assai. (♩=168)

A
(Мал. Фл.)
(Kl. Fl.)
a 2
A

mf
poco
a
cresc.
p

Piatti
pizz.
pizz.

sf
sf
sf
f
arco
arco

B
p
cre
pizz.
arco

scen
do
mp
mf
f
ff
cresc.
Piatti

mf
cre - scen - do
cre - scen - do
cre - scen - do
cre - scen - do
cre - scen -
cre - scen -
cresc.
cresc.
cresc.
cresc.
mp
cresc.
cre - scen -
mf
cresc.
mf
cresc.
mf
cresc.
mf
cresc.
mf
cresc.

ff
mf
do
cresc.
mp
f

C
cre - scen - do
ff
f
P.
G. C.
C

D
D

cresc.
ff
f

ФИНАЛЬНЫЙ ВАЛЬСЪ И АПОѲЕОЗЪ. №15. VALSE FINALE ET APOTHEOSE.
Tempo di Valse.
Flauto I.
Flauto II.
Piccolo.
2 Oboi.
Corno Inglese.
2 Clarinetti in B.
Clar. basso in B.
Fagotti.
Corni in F I. II. III. IV.
Trombe in B.
Tromboni Tenori.
Tr. Basso e Tuba.
Timp. in F, B, Es.
Piatti e gr. Cassa.
Celesta.
Tempo di Valse.
Arpe I e II.
Violino I.
div.
unis.
Violino II.
unis.
Viole.
Cello.
C-Basso.
Tempo di Valse.

-scen - do
ff
f
mf
div.
unis.

cresc.
cre - scen - do
cre - scen - do
div.
div.

A
fff
fff
fff
fff
fff
fff
fff
a 2
fff
ff
ff
f
sfp
f
f
f
f
unis.
unis.
A

a 2
sfp
f
f

fff
a 2
ff
f
sfp
ff

B
a 2
a 2
sfp
f
f
f
f
B

Piatti.
Cassa
div.
div.
unis.
unis.
ff
sf
mp
cresc.

div.
div.
unis.
unis.

C
sf
mp
cresc.
ff
div.
C

pizz.
pizz.
pizz.
pizz.
pizz.

D
cresc.
ff
mf
f
Celesta.
Arpe I e II.
arco
2 Soli.
p
pp
D

Celesta.
Arpe I e II.
V. I.
V. II.
Cel.
C. B.
E
Fl. I.
Piccolo.
8
Cl. I.
Cl. II.
(NOTA. Cl. basso tacet.)
Celesta.
Arpe I e II.
2 Soli.
E

Cl.I.
Cl.II.(Cl Basso tacet.)
a 2
cantabile
cantabile
cantabile
cantabile
Tutti
Tutti.
Tutti.
Tutti
Tutti
pizz.
Tutti.

a 2
Cl. I e II
Cl. Basso.
p
p
p
p

Cl. I e II.
a 2
mp
poco cresc.
p

Cl. I. II.
arco
pizz.
F

Cl. I e II.

Cl. I e II.
Cl. bas.
cre
scen
cresc.

G
scen - do
div.
arco
G

sf
mp
cresc.
unis.

div.
div.
unis.
unis.

H
pp
cre - scen - do
poco a poco
div.
H

fff
a 2
P.
fff
ff G.C.
I

fff

a 2

APOTHEOSIS.

Апоѳеозъ.
L'Apotheose.
Molto meno.(♩=144)
K
p
pp
sffp
pizz.
Molto meno.(♩=144)
K

D
arco
arco
D

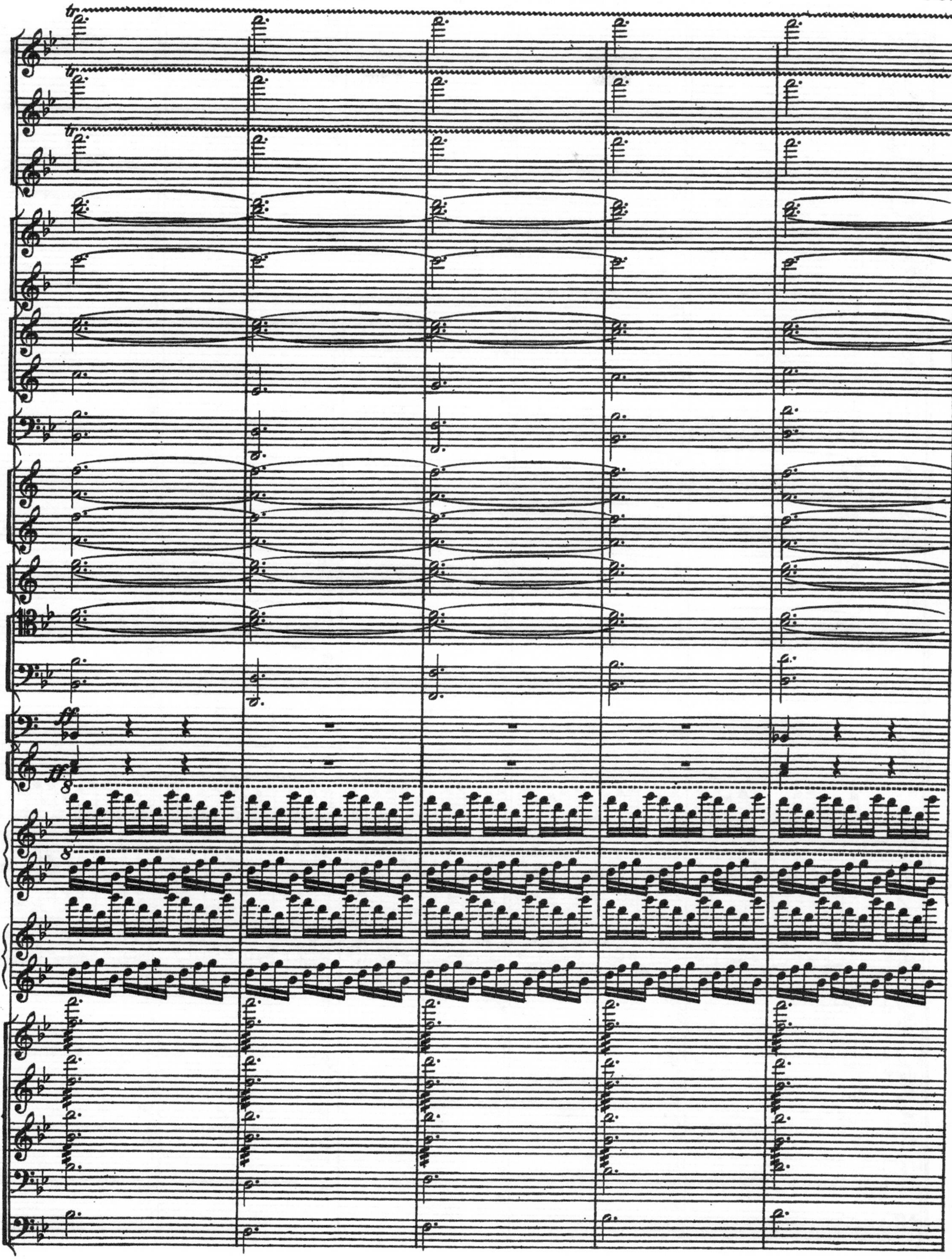
tr
tr
tr
ff
ff
8
8

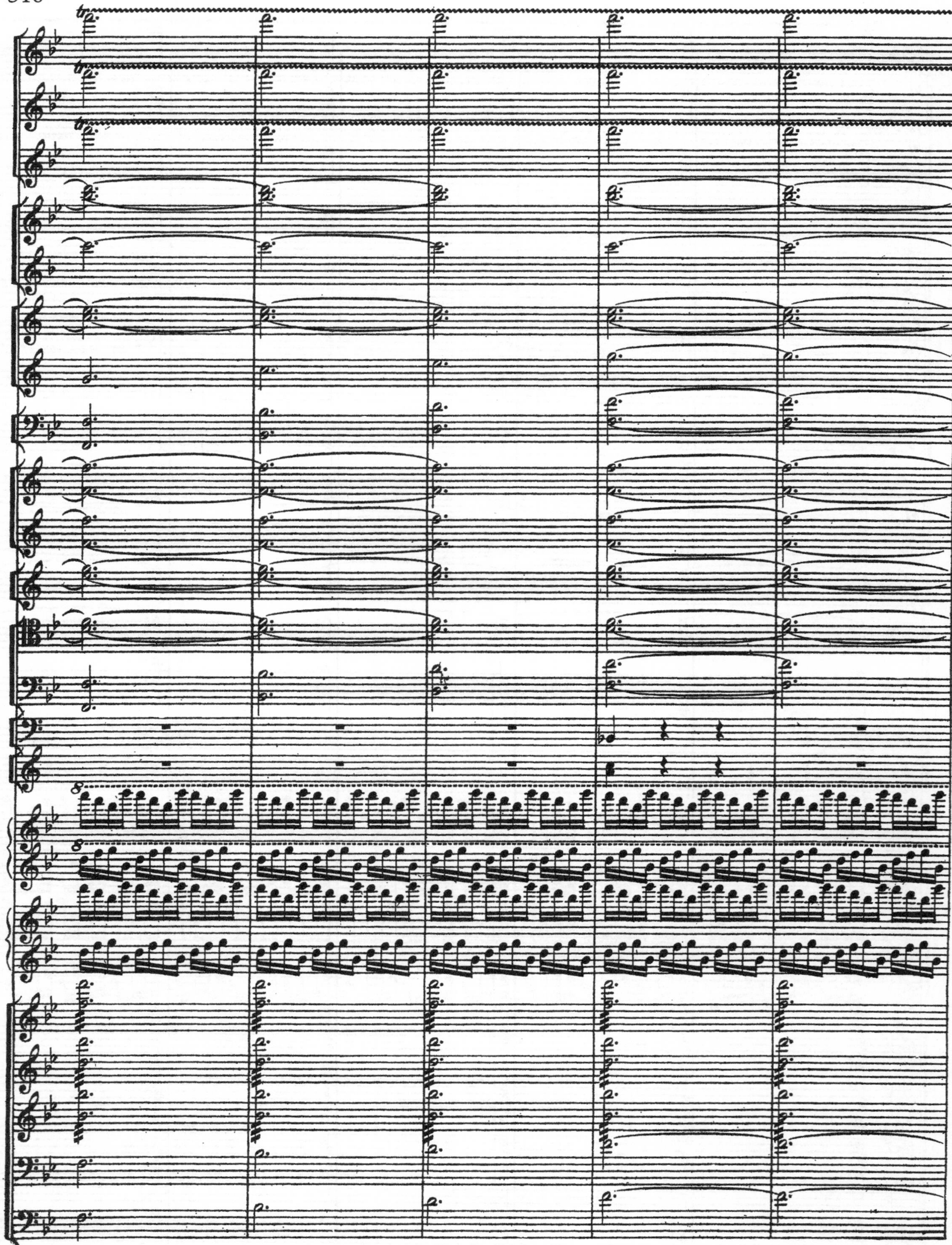

tr
tr
tr
fff
8
8

Dover Orchestral Scores

Bach, Johann Sebastian, COMPLETE CONCERTI FOR SOLO KEYBOARD AND ORCHESTRA IN FULL SCORE. Bach's seven complete concerti for solo keyboard and orchestra in full score from the authoritative Bach-Gesellschaft edition. 206pp. 9 x 12. 0-486-24929-8

Bach, Johann Sebastian, THE SIX BRANDENBURG CONCERTOS AND THE FOUR ORCHESTRAL SUITES IN FULL SCORE. Complete standard Bach-Gesellschaft editions in large, clear format. Study score. 273pp. 9 x 12. 0-486-23376-6

Bach, Johann Sebastian, THE THREE VIOLIN CONCERTI IN FULL SCORE. Concerto in A Minor, BWV 1041; Concerto in E Major, BWV 1042; and Concerto for Two Violins in D Minor, BWV 1043. Bach-Gesellschaft editions. 64pp. 9⅜ x 12¼. 0-486-25124-1

Beethoven, Ludwig van, COMPLETE PIANO CONCERTOS IN FULL SCORE. Complete scores of five great Beethoven piano concertos, with all cadenzas as he wrote them, reproduced from authoritative Breitkopf & Härtel edition. New Table of Contents. 384pp. 9⅜ x 12¼. 0-486-24563-2

Beethoven, Ludwig van, SIX GREAT OVERTURES IN FULL SCORE. Six staples of the orchestral repertoire from authoritative Breitkopf & Härtel edition. *Leonore Overtures,* Nos. 1–3; Overtures to *Coriolanus, Egmont, Fidelio.* 288pp. 9 x 12. 0-486-24789-9

Beethoven, Ludwig van, SYMPHONIES NOS. 1, 2, 3, AND 4 IN FULL SCORE. Republication of H. Litolff edition. 272pp. 9 x 12. 0-486-26033-X

Beethoven, Ludwig van, SYMPHONIES NOS. 5, 6 AND 7 IN FULL SCORE, Ludwig van Beethoven. Republication of H. Litolff edition. 272pp. 9 x 12. 0-486-26034-8

Beethoven, Ludwig van, SYMPHONIES NOS. 8 AND 9 IN FULL SCORE. Republication of H. Litolff edition. 256pp. 9 x 12. 0-486-26035-6

Beethoven, Ludwig van; Mendelssohn, Felix; and Tchaikovsky, Peter Ilyitch, GREAT ROMANTIC VIOLIN CONCERTI IN FULL SCORE. The Beethoven Op. 61, Mendelssohn Op. 64 and Tchaikovsky Op. 35 concertos reprinted from Breitkopf & Härtel editions. 224pp. 9 x 12. 0-486-24989-1

Borodin, Alexander, SYMPHONY NO. 2 IN B MINOR IN FULL SCORE. Rescored after its disastrous debut, the four movements offer a unified construction of dramatic contrasts in mood, color, and tempo. A beloved example of Russian nationalist music of the Romantic period. viii+152pp. 9 x 12. 0-486-44120-2

Brahms, Johannes, COMPLETE CONCERTI IN FULL SCORE. Piano Concertos Nos. 1 and 2; Violin Concerto, Op. 77; Concerto for Violin and Cello, Op. 102. Definitive Breitkopf & Härtel edition. 352pp. 9⅜ x 12¼. 0-486-24170-X

Brahms, Johannes, COMPLETE SYMPHONIES. Full orchestral scores in one volume. No. 1 in C Minor, Op. 68; No. 2 in D Major, Op. 73; No. 3 in F Major, Op. 90; and No. 4 in E Minor, Op. 98. Reproduced from definitive Vienna Gesellschaft der Musikfreunde edition. Study score. 344pp. 9 x 12. 0-486-23053-8

Brahms, Johannes, THREE ORCHESTRAL WORKS IN FULL SCORE: Academic Festival Overture, Tragic Overture and Variations on a Theme by Joseph Haydn. Reproduced from the authoritative Breitkopf & Härtel edition three of Brahms's great orchestral favorites. Editor's commentary in German and English. 112pp. 9⅜ x 12¼. 0-486-24637-X

Chopin, Frédéric, THE PIANO CONCERTOS IN FULL SCORE. The authoritative Breitkopf & Härtel full-score edition in one volume; Piano Concertos No. 1 in E Minor and No. 2 in F Minor. 176pp. 9 x 12. 0-486-25835-1

Corelli, Arcangelo, COMPLETE CONCERTI GROSSI IN FULL SCORE. All 12 concerti in the famous late nineteenth-century edition prepared by violinist Joseph Joachim and musicologist Friedrich Chrysander. 240pp. 8⅜ x 11¼. 0-486-25606-5

Debussy, Claude, THREE GREAT ORCHESTRAL WORKS IN FULL SCORE. Three of the Impressionist's most-recorded, most-performed favorites: *Prélude à l'Après-midi d'un Faune, Nocturnes,* and *La Mer.* Reprinted from early French editions. 279pp. 9 x 12. 0-486-24441-5

Dvořák, Antonín, SERENADE NO. 1, OP. 22, AND SERENADE NO. 2, OP. 44, IN FULL SCORE. Two works typified by elegance of form, intense harmony, rhythmic variety, and uninhibited emotionalism. 96pp. 9 x 12. 0-486-41895-2

Dvořák, Antonín, SYMPHONY NO. 8 IN G MAJOR, OP. 88, SYMPHONY NO. 9 IN E MINOR, OP. 95 ("NEW WORLD") IN FULL SCORE. Two celebrated symphonies by the great Czech composer, the Eighth and the immensely popular Ninth, "From the New World," in one volume. 272pp. 9 x 12. 0-486-24749-X

Elgar, Edward, CELLO CONCERTO IN E MINOR, OP. 85, IN FULL SCORE. A tour de force for any cellist, this frequently performed work is widely regarded as an elegy for a lost world. Melodic and evocative, it exhibits a remarkable scope, ranging from tragic passion to buoyant optimism. Reproduced from an authoritative source. 112pp. 8⅜ x 11. 0-486-41896-0

Franck, César, SYMPHONY IN D MINOR IN FULL SCORE. Superb, authoritative edition of Franck's only symphony, an often-performed and recorded masterwork of late French romantic style. 160pp. 9 x 12. 0-486-25373-2

Handel, George Frideric, COMPLETE CONCERTI GROSSI IN FULL SCORE. Monumental Opus 6 Concerti Grossi, Opus 3 and "Alexander's Feast" Concerti Grossi–19 in all–reproduced from the most authoritative edition. 258pp. 9⅜ x 12¼. 0-486-24187-4

Handel, George Frideric, WATER MUSIC AND MUSIC FOR THE ROYAL FIREWORKS IN FULL SCORE. Full scores of two of the most popular Baroque orchestral works performed today–reprinted from the definitive Deutsche Handelgesellschaft edition. Total of 96pp. 8⅛ x 11. 0-486-25070-9

Haydn, Joseph, SYMPHONIES 88–92 IN FULL SCORE: The Haydn Society Edition. Full score of symphonies Nos. 88 through 92. Large, readable noteheads, ample margins for fingerings, etc., and extensive Editor's Commentary. 304pp. 9 x 12. (Available in U.S. only) 0-486-24445-8

Mahler, Gustav, DAS LIED VON DER ERDE IN FULL SCORE. Mahler's masterpiece, a fusion of song and symphony, reprinted from the original 1912 Universal Edition. English translations of song texts. 160pp. 9 x 12. 0-486-25657-X

Mahler, Gustav, SYMPHONIES NOS. 1 AND 2 IN FULL SCORE. Unabridged, authoritative Austrian editions of Symphony No. 1 in D Major ("Titan") and Symphony No. 2 in C Minor ("Resurrection"). 384pp. 8⅛ x 11. 0-486-25473-9

Mahler, Gustav, SYMPHONIES NOS. 3 AND 4 IN FULL SCORE. Two brilliantly contrasting masterworks–one scored for a massive ensemble, the other for small orchestra and soloist–reprinted from authoritative Viennese editions. 368pp. 9⅜ x 12¼. 0-486-26166-2

Mahler, Gustav, SYMPHONY NO. 8 IN FULL SCORE. Authoritative edition of massive, complex "Symphony of a Thousand." Scored for orchestra, eight solo voices, double chorus, boys' choir and organ. Reprint of Izdatel'stvo "Muzyka," Moscow, edition. Translation of texts. 272pp. 9⅜ x 12¼. 0-486-26022-4

Mendelssohn, Felix, MAJOR ORCHESTRAL WORKS IN FULL SCORE. Considered to be Mendelssohn's finest orchestral works, here in one volume are the complete *Midsummer Night's Dream; Hebrides Overture; Calm Sea and Prosperous Voyage Overture;* Symphony No. 3 in A ("Scottish"); and Symphony No. 4 in A ("Italian"). Breitkopf & Härtel edition. Study score. 406pp. 9 x 12. 0-486-23184-4

Dover Orchestral Scores

Mozart, Wolfgang Amadeus, CONCERTI FOR WIND INSTRUMENTS IN FULL SCORE. Exceptional volume contains ten pieces for orchestra and wind instruments and includes some of Mozart's finest, most popular music. 272pp. 9⅜ x 12¼. 0-486-25228-0

Mozart, Wolfgang Amadeus, LATER SYMPHONIES. Full orchestral scores to last symphonies (Nos. 35–41) reproduced from definitive Breitkopf & Härtel Complete Works edition. Study score. 285pp. 9 x 12. 0-486-23052-X

Mozart, Wolfgang Amadeus, PIANO CONCERTOS NOS. 1–6 IN FULL SCORE. Reproduced complete and unabridged from the authoritative Breitkopf & Hartel Complete Works edition, it offers a revealing look at the development of a budding master. x+198pp. 9⅜ x 12¼. 0-486-44191-1

Mozart, Wolfgang Amadeus, PIANO CONCERTOS NOS. 11–16 IN FULL SCORE. Authoritative Breitkopf & Härtel edition of six staples of the concerto repertoire, including Mozart's cadenzas for Nos. 12–16. 256pp. 9⅜ x 12¼. 0-486-25468-2

Mozart, Wolfgang Amadeus, PIANO CONCERTOS NOS. 17–22 IN FULL SCORE. Six complete piano concertos in full score, with Mozart's own cadenzas for Nos. 17–19. Breitkopf & Härtel edition. Study score. 370pp. 9⅜ x 12¼. 0-486-23599-8

Mozart, Wolfgang Amadeus, PIANO CONCERTOS NOS. 23–27 IN FULL SCORE. Mozart's last five piano concertos in full score, plus cadenzas for Nos. 23 and 27, and the Concert Rondo in D Major, K.382. Breitkopf & Härtel edition. Study score. 310pp. 9⅜ x 12¼. 0-486-23600-5

Mozart, Wolfgang Amadeus, 17 DIVERTIMENTI FOR VARIOUS INSTRUMENTS. Sparkling pieces of great vitality and brilliance from 1771 to 1779; consecutively numbered from 1 to 17. Reproduced from definitive Breitkopf & Härtel Complete Works edition. Study score. 241pp. 9⅜ x 12¼. 0-486-23862-8

Mozart, Wolfgang Amadeus, THE VIOLIN CONCERTI AND THE SINFONIA CONCERTANTE, K.364, IN FULL SCORE. All five violin concerti and famed double concerto reproduced from authoritative Breitkopf & Härtel Complete Works Edition. 208pp. 9⅜ x 12¼. 0-486-25169-1

Paganini, Nicolo and Wieniawski, Henri, PAGANINI'S VIOLIN CONCERTO NO. 1 IN D MAJOR, OP. 6, AND WIENIAWSKI'S VIOLIN CONCERTO NO. 2 IN D MINOR, OP. 22, IN FULL SCORE. This outstanding new edition brings together two of the most popular and most performed violin concertos of the Romantic repertoire in one convenient, moderately priced volume. 208pp. 8⅜ x 11. 0-486-43151-7

Ravel, Maurice, DAPHNIS AND CHLOE IN FULL SCORE. Definitive full-score edition of Ravel's rich musical setting of a Greek fable by Longus is reprinted here from the original French edition. 320pp. 9⅜ x 12¼. (Not available in France or Germany) 0-486-25826-2

Ravel, Maurice, LE TOMBEAU DE COUPERIN and VALSES NOBLES ET SENTIMENTALES IN FULL SCORE. *Le Tombeau de Couperin* consists of "Prelude," "Forlane," "Menuet," and "Rigaudon"; the uninterrupted 8 waltzes of *Valses Nobles et Sentimentales* abound with lilting rhythms and unexpected harmonic subtleties. 144pp. 9⅜ x 12¼. (Not available in France or Germany) 0-486-41898-7

Ravel, Maurice, RAPSODIE ESPAGNOLE, MOTHER GOOSE and PAVANE FOR A DEAD PRINCESS IN FULL SCORE. Full authoritative scores of 3 enormously popular works by the great French composer, each rich in orchestral settings. 160pp. 9⅜ x 12¼. 0-486-41899-5

Saint-Saens, Camille, DANSE MACABRE AND HAVANAISE FOR VIOLIN AND ORCHESTRA IN FULL SCORE. Two of Saint-Saens' most popular works appear in this affordable volume: the symphonic poem about the dance of death, *Danse Macabre,* and *Havanaise,* a piece inspired by a Cuban dance that highlights its languid mood with bursts of virtuosity. iv+92pp. 9 x 12. 0-486-44147-4

Schubert, Franz, FOUR SYMPHONIES IN FULL SCORE. Schubert's four most popular symphonies: No. 4 in C Minor ("Tragic"); No. 5 in B-flat Major; No. 8 in B Minor ("Unfinished"); and No. 9 in C Major ("Great"). Breitkopf & Härtel edition. Study score. 261pp. 9⅜ x 12¼. 0-486-23681-1

Schubert, Franz, SYMPHONY NO. 3 IN D MAJOR AND SYMPHONY NO. 6 IN C MAJOR IN FULL SCORE. The former is scored for 12 wind instruments and timpani; the latter is known as "The Little Symphony in C" to distinguish it from Symphony No. 9, "The Great Symphony in C." Authoritative editions. 128pp. 9⅜ x 12¼. 0-486-42134-1

Schumann, Robert, COMPLETE SYMPHONIES IN FULL SCORE. No. 1 in B-flat Major, Op. 38 ("Spring"); No. 2 in C Major, Op. 61; No. 3 in E-flat Major, Op. 97 ("Rhenish"); and No. 4 in D Minor, Op. 120. Breitkopf & Härtel editions. Study score. 416pp. 9⅜ x 12¼. 0-486-24013-4

Strauss, Johann, Jr., THE GREAT WALTZES IN FULL SCORE. Complete scores of eight melodic masterpieces: "The Beautiful Blue Danube," "Emperor Waltz," "Tales of the Vienna Woods," "Wiener Blut," and four more. Authoritative editions. 336pp. 8⅞ x 11¼. 0-486-26009-7

Strauss, Richard, TONE POEMS, SERIES I: DON JUAN, TOD UND VERKLARUNG, and DON QUIXOTE IN FULL SCORE. Three of the most often performed and recorded works in entire orchestral repertoire, reproduced in full score from original editions. 286pp. 9⅜ x 12¼. (Available in U.S. only) 0-486-23754-0

Strauss, Richard, TONE POEMS, SERIES II: TILL EULENSPIEGELS LUSTIGE STREICHE, "ALSO SPRACH ZARATHUSTRA," and EIN HELDENLEBEN IN FULL SCORE. Three important orchestral works, including very popular *Till Eulenspiegel's Merry Pranks,* reproduced in full score from original editions. Study score. 315pp. 9⅜ x 12¼. (Available in U.S. only) 0-486-23755-9

Stravinsky, Igor, THE FIREBIRD IN FULL SCORE (Original 1910 Version). Inexpensive edition of modern masterpiece, renowned for brilliant orchestration, glowing color. Authoritative Russian edition. 176pp. 9⅜ x 12¼. (Available in U.S. only) 0-486-25535-2

Stravinsky, Igor, PETRUSHKA IN FULL SCORE: Original Version. Full-score edition of Stravinsky's masterful score for the great Ballets Russes 1911 production of *Petrushka.* 160pp. 9⅜ x 12¼. (Available in U.S. only) 0-486-25680-4

Stravinsky, Igor, THE RITE OF SPRING IN FULL SCORE. Full-score edition of most famous musical work of the 20th century, created as a ballet score for Diaghilev's Ballets Russes. 176pp. 9⅜ x 12¼. (Available in U.S. only) 0-486-25857-2

Tchaikovsky, Peter Ilyitch, FOURTH, FIFTH AND SIXTH SYMPHONIES IN FULL SCORE. Complete orchestral scores of Symphony No. 4 in F Minor, Op. 36; Symphony No. 5 in E Minor, Op. 64; Symphony No. 6 in B Minor, "Pathetique," Op. 74. Study score. Breitkopf & Härtel editions. 480pp. 9⅜ x 12¼. 0-486-23861-X

Tchaikovsky, Peter Ilyitch, NUTCRACKER SUITE IN FULL SCORE. Among the most popular ballet pieces ever created; available in a complete, inexpensive, high-quality score to study and enjoy. 128pp. 9 x 12. 0-486-25379-1

von Weber, Carl Maria, GREAT OVERTURES IN FULL SCORE. Overtures to *Oberon, Der Freischutz, Euryanthe* and *Preciosa* reprinted from authoritative Breitkopf & Härtel editions. 112pp. 9 x 12. 0-486-25225-6